D0522072

Lifeboat
In Danger's Hour

Lifeboat

In Danger's Hour

Patrick Howarth

Foreword by Clare Francis

HAMLYN
London · New York · Sydney · Toronto

To Joan Davies, Heather Deane, Shelley Ginever, David Jarman,
Ray Kipling, Richard Mann and Edward Wake-Walker, in gratitude.

half-title page
St Mary's, Scilly Isles, lifeboat
on service during the Fastnet
Race in August 1979.

title pages
Penzance lifeboat *Dora* saved
the crew of the *Jeune Hortense*,
a brigantine wrecked off
Eastern Green, Penzance,
in 1888.

The photographs in this book (the majority of which are from the
collection of the RNLI) are reproduced by permission of the following:

Aberdeen Journals 109 bottom; H. E. Appleton 109 top; Associated Press
11 bottom; S. Bennetts 90 top, 90 bottom, 91 top, 91 bottom; Central
Press 126; Cork Examiner 56–57; Daily Mirror 94 top; George Dey 62;
A. M. Ferry 100; Fox Photos 20 bottom; F. E. Gibson 2–3; Ambrose
Greenway 97, 117 bottom; Peter Hadfield 24 bottom, 28, 77 top right,
98–99, 105 top, 115, 133 bottom; Herald Express (Torquay) 74; HMS
Daedalus 124; HMS Gannet 69, 70–71; HMS Osprey 88–89; Hull Daily
Mail 104; Irish Press 30 top; Keystone Press Agency 83 top, 112 bottom;
Basil Kidd 108, 116; London Express Pictures 23 top centre; Lowestoft
Journal 122; Campbell MacCallum 15, 29 top, 31, 32–33, 34 top, 34
bottom, 35, 36 top, 36 bottom, 37 top, 37 bottom, 63 top, 123 bottom,
127; J. P. Morris 96 bottom; Margaret Murray 77 top left; Namemakers
Ltd 120; Newcastle Chronicle and Journal 123 top; North Eastern Press
(Fraserburgh) 125; Observer 75; David Parker 78–79; Press Association
72; Anthony Reynolds 54 bottom; RNAS Culdrose 1; Roger Smith 67
bottom; Frank Meadow Sutcliffe Collection 93 centre, 111; The Times 94
bottom; David Trotter 105 bottom; US Coast Guard 131, 132 top;
Valentine (Dundee) 7; Reg Vincent 23 top left; Ray Warner 83 bottom;
Western Mail and Echo (Cardiff) 24 top; Charles White 23 bottom; R. J.
Wilson 117 top, 118–119.

Published by the Hamlyn Publishing Group Limited
Astronaut House, Hounslow Road, Feltham, Middlesex.
First published 1981
© Copyright The Royal National Lifeboat Institution 1981

ISBN 0 600 34959 4
Typeset by Fakenham Press Limited, Fakenham, England
Printed in Great Britain.

All rights reserved. No part of this publication may be
reproduced, stored in a retrieval system, or transmitted,
in any form or by any means, electronic, mechanical,
photocopying, recording or otherwise, without the permission
of The Hamlyn Publishing Group Limited and the copyright holder.

Contents

Foreword

Contrary to the widely-held belief, it is not the ocean that presents the greatest danger to ships and small boats, it is coastal waters – and particularly those around Britain. Lying in the path of some of the worst weather in the world, Britain's rugged western coast is an uncompromising lee shore which lies in wait for the unwary. To the east the shallow, choppy North Sea can produce waves of up to sixty feet during winter storms. And the many ships which make their way up the English Channel have to negotiate the vicious rocks of Scilly and Cornwall before entering the hazardous Dover Strait, one of the busiest waterways in the world.

For centuries Britain's coastal waters were a graveyard for ships and men. In poor visibility ships were virtually blind and many a fine vessel was driven on to the rocks, her crew unaware of the proximity of land. In bad weather, sailing ships were particularly vulnerable to the dangers of the lee shore and, despite all attempts to claw to windward, would sometimes be pushed remorselessly towards the land. Those in difficulties near land did at least have the slim hope of being swept on to a beach – those in distress out at sea had little chance of being saved.

It was not that people did not want to attempt rescue: those who live and work by the sea have always recognized the need to help each other; and the harshness and isolation of the life forms a strong bond even between strangers. However, until the lifeboat service developed, rescue attempts were often in vain; without suitable boats and equipment it was difficult to save people even when shipwrecked near the shore. In the wake of terrible disasters or frequent losses, money was raised to build special life-saving boats and the idea of a voluntary service was born; and those who sailed in British waters began to count themselves lucky indeed. Whatever the weather, whatever the conditions they could be certain that a call for help would be answered.

Today modern navigational aids enable the smallest of vessels to find their way in thick fog. Nevertheless the lifeboat service is just as busy as it was a hundred years ago because of the vast increase in the number of ships, fishing craft and pleasure boats. Despite radar and gyrocompass, lighthouse and chart, the sea still manages to keep the upper hand; error, human or technical, can put the best-equipped vessels in danger.

The lifeboat service holds a very special place in the affections of the British people. Our history is bound inexorably to the sea and we are more than ever dependent on it for the carriage of our food and raw materials. We are justly proud that our country should have produced a voluntary service of men and women who endanger their lives to save those who work and live on the sea. Increasingly the service also helps those who go to sea for pleasure, myself included. Like most small-boat sailors, I very much hope that I shall never have occasion to call out the lifeboat, but if I do run out of luck – if my boat is dismasted, holed and sinking fast – I pray that it will happen in British waters.

The story of the lifeboat service is not just a tale of bravery (although there is plenty of that) but of endurance, tenacity and faith. To the men clinging to a life-raft the knowledge that the lifeboat will keep looking for him, perhaps for days, is vital; it gives him an essential thread of hope. The dramatic rescue justly receives acclaim but the less publicized activities of the service – the long weary searches, the escorting of disabled vessels, the false alarms – these are the thankless tasks which may keep the gallant lifeboatmen at sea for days in the most appalling conditions.

The story of the service is also one of organization: of building, maintaining and running the boats to the highest standard. Here too no effort is spared to make the service the best available. The development of the RNLI, from its tentative beginnings to the major national organization it is today, is a triumph of determination and national will. Long may it continue.

Clare Francis

The origins of the lifeboat service

The readiness of men and women to put out to sea in boats, even at the risk of their own lives, in order to save others is one of the most attractive human characteristics. Examples of it have been recorded in different centuries, in different continents and at different levels of civilization.

It is commonly believed that before the late eighteenth century ships round the coasts of Britain were at the mercy of wreckers, who were interested only in gain. Plunder from ships did provide the inhabitants of coastal towns and villages with occasional bounty. There may have been some truth in the stories of lanterns being tied to cows' tails in order to guide ships on to the rocks. Yet there are also numerous authenticated records of rescues, some of them carried out by those very boatmen whose livelihood depended largely on the proceeds of shipwreck. When thirteen warships were lost off the coast of Kent in a hurricane in 1703 sixty-four men were saved by one Deal lugger and two hundred more by other boats. Deal was well known as a centre of the salvage business.

Rescue at sea is often a spontaneous act. Prince Peter Kropotkin, the great Russian anarchist, believed it provided convincing evidence to support his theory of mutual aid. He had developed this theory after a study of animal life during an extensive tour of Eastern Siberia, and after he settled in England he repeatedly cited the achievements of the crews of the Royal National Lifeboat Institution as supreme examples of mutual aid in practice among human beings. Partly because of this instinctive, spontaneous element in sea rescue, and partly because rescues are often associated with other activities, such as salvage of property, it is difficult to establish with certainty when and where organized life-saving at sea began. There is even doubt about the site of the world's first lifeboat station.

There have been reports circulating in the western world for some time that rescue boats operated at the mouth of the Yangtse River in the mid-eighteenth century. No western historian has succeeded in authenticating these reports, and attempts made in the West to obtain supporting evidence from China have hitherto failed.

Until recently it was widely accepted that the world's first lifeboat station was established at Bamburgh in Northumberland. A document dated Christmas Eve 1771 described an elaborate organization in Bamburgh Castle for warning ships of danger and for helping shipwrecked mariners. Two horsemen were instructed to patrol the coast from sunset to sunrise during periods of storms, and a large 'speaking trumpet' was provided for communicating with ships.

This organization was controlled by the trustees of a charity known as the Crewe Trust. The chief administrator of the trust, Dr John Sharp, Archdeacon of Northumberland and perpetual curate of Bamburgh, learnt of some experiments being carried out

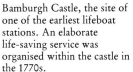

Bamburgh Castle, the site of one of the earliest lifeboat stations. An elaborate life-saving service was organised within the castle in the 1770s.

by an inventive coach-builder named Lionel Lukin. The aim of these experiments was to provide a boat which would not sink or, as Lukin happily put it, would be 'unimmergible'. Sharp asked Lukin to convert a fishing coble according to his new principle. Lukin agreed, and the arrival in Bamburgh in 1786 of a converted coble to be used exclusively for life-saving gave Bamburgh its claim to have had the world's first lifeboat station.

A group of retired lifeboatmen from Lowestoft in the last century. When the picture was taken their combined ages totalled 312. Left to right: William Hook (75), James Burwood (76), Thomas Coleman (80) and Matthew Coleman (81).

This claim began to be disputed in the late 1970s, when Mrs Barbara Yorke, a native of Formby in Lancashire, assisted by her husband, Dr Reginald Yorke, investigated certain municipal records in Liverpool. One council minute dated 5th March 1777 – that is to say nearly ten years before Lukin's coble was sent to Bamburgh – gave instructions for repairs to be carried out to 'the boat, which was formerly ordered to be built and kept at Formby in readiness to fetch any shipwrecked persons from the banks'. A minute recorded nearly a month later gave instructions for the 'sailor' in charge of the boat, Richard Scarisbrick, and his crew to be 'handsomely rewarded for any good services done'.

Possibly therefore Richard Scarisbrick, of whom nothing else appears to be known, was the world's first lifeboat coxswain. It is of course not impossible that other lifeboat stations will be discovered to have existed before Formby. Although the British have generally been accepted as pioneers in the organization of saving life in coastal waters, such stations may well be outside Britain.

The distinction of being the inventor of the lifeboat itself is also one to which there is more than one claimant. In 1765 the French Controller-General of Bridges and Embankments, M. de Bernières, carried out some experiments with a boat which he considered unsinkable. The boat was fitted with air cases at stem and stern and could right herself quickly when overturned. Trials were carried out before a distinguished gathering at the gate of the Invalides in Paris in August 1777. They seem to have been fairly successful, but as there is no evidence that the boat was ever used for life-saving de Bernières can hardly be considered to have invented the lifeboat.

Lukin seems to have had little doubt

The former lifeboathouse at Formby, Lancashire, in 1933, showing how the sands had begun to take over. The Formby station may have been the first in the world, but it was closed down in 1919.

about his own claims. He was a prolific inventor. Among his other original creations were a rain gauge, a new method of ventilating ships and a reclining bed for invalids. Yet it was his experiments with rescue boats to which he attached the greatest importance. He died in his ninety-second year at Hythe in Kent, and the inscription on his tombstone, which he had himself composed, included the words: 'This Lionel Lukin was the first who built a Life-boat, and was the original inventor of that principle of safety.'

The earliest boats which Lukin made available for life-saving were conversions of existing boats. The rescue boat stationed at Formby may not have even been a conversion and was probably a conventional Mersey gig. By contrast a boat which came into service at North Shields in 1790, following a major disaster, was designed from the outset for life-saving and for this reason may be considered the first true lifeboat. She was appropriately named *Original*, served for some forty years and helped to save hundreds of lives.

The disaster which led to the building of the *Original* occurred at the mouth of the Tyne in March 1789. A ship named the *Adventure* was wrecked, and her crew could be clearly seen from the shore as they dropped helplessly from the rigging into the sea.

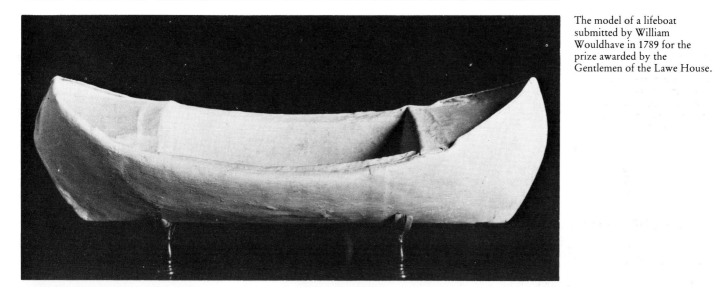

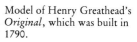

THE INVENTION,

PRINCIPLES OF CONSTRUCTION,

AND USES OF

UNIMMERGIBLE BOATS,

STATED IN A LETTER TO HIS ROYAL HIGHNESS

THE PRINCE OF WALES.

BY LIONEL LUKIN.

LONDON:
PRINTED FOR THE AUTHOR,
By J. Nichols and Son, Red Lion Passage, Fleet Street ;
AND SOLD BY T. BECKETT, PALL MALL ; T. EGERTON,
WHITEHALL ; AND J. ASPERNE, CORNHILL.

1806.

How Lionel Lukin obtained the patronage of the future King George IV, with diagrams of the boat he designed.

The model of a lifeboat submitted by William Wouldhave in 1789 for the prize awarded by the Gentlemen of the Lawe House.

Model of Henry Greathead's *Original*, which was built in 1790.

opposite top
The City of London Tavern in Billingsgate Street, which was the site of the meeting held on 4th March 1824 at which it was resolved to form the body now known as the Royal National Lifeboat Institution.

opposite bottom
Crew of the Douglas pulling lifeboat. In the late 1860s Charles Dibdin, who worked in the Savings Bank of the General Post Office, established a fund, of which he became honorary secretary in 1870. Its aim was to raise money for new lifeboats from voluntary gifts made by civil servants. Over the years the Civil Service and Post Office Lifeboat Fund has provided nearly forty new lifeboats, including the pulling lifeboat at Douglas shown here. Dibdin himself was Secretary of the RNLI from 1883 to 1910.

Members of a private club who called themselves the Gentlemen of the Lawe House thereupon offered a prize for a design of a lifeboat. The best submitted was deemed to be that of William Wouldhave, the parish clerk of South Shields, though the adjudicating committee saw fit to award him only half the prize of two guineas offered. Two members of the committee named Rockwood and Fairles modified Wouldhave's design, and the actual construction of the boat was entrusted to Henry Greathead, a respected local boat-builder.

Wouldhave's tombstone also proclaims him to have been the inventor of the lifeboat, but it was Greathead who received the material rewards. Parliament voted him £1200, and the Society of Arts, Trinity House and Lloyd's all awarded him substantial sums.

.   .   .

Although the origins of the lifeboat and of lifeboat stations can be the subject of dispute, with the possibility that new evidence may still be found to upset existing theories, there seems little doubt about how and through whose agency the world's first national lifeboat organization came into being.

In the first quarter of the nineteenth century a number of lifeboats were brought into service in Britain and elsewhere. They were manned and administered through local enterprise. In Britain many of the lifeboats were paid for by Lloyd's, an example of farsightedness and philanthropy which caused King George V, when laying the foundation stone of a new building for Lloyd's in 1925, to go so far as to state: 'It is not a mere coincidence that we owe the institution of our lifeboat service to Lloyd's.' In the first decade of the nineteenth century the body which later became known as the Dublin Port and Docks Board controlled a number of Irish lifeboat stations. The second Duke of Northumberland paid for several lifeboats, and it is a revealing reflection on British commercial interests at the time that one of these was stationed at Oporto in Portugal long before a national lifeboat organization came into being in Britain.

One of the earlier lifeboat stations was established at Douglas, Isle of Man, in 1802. Among those who served with distinction in the Douglas lifeboat was a man of rich imagination, great physical courage and a tragic inability to manage his own financial affairs. This was Sir William Hillary, the principal founder of the body which became known as the Royal National Lifeboat Institution.

Hillary settled in the Isle of Man partly in order to escape creditors and partly because he had eloped and contracted a marriage which may well have been bigamous. His creditors were to pursue him beyond the grave, and soon after he died his body was removed from its coffin, possibly to be sold to medical practitioners. Yet in his lifetime he helped to save more than three hundred people while serving in the Douglas lifeboat. On one occasion he was washed overboard and had six of his ribs fractured. He could

Sir William Hillary (1771–1847), founder of the RNLI.

Inscription on the tomb of Sir William and Lady Hillary in St George's Churchyard, Douglas, Isle of Man.

TO THE HONOURED MEMORY OF
LIEUT. COLONEL SIR WILLIAM HILLARY, BT
OF YORKSHIRE, ESSEX, AND THE ISLE OF MAN.
LIEUTENANT TURCOPOLIER OF THE ORDER OF THE KNIGHTS OF ST JOHN OF JERUSALEM,
BORN 1771. DIED 1847.
SOLDIER, AUTHOR, PHILANTHROPIST,
HE FOUNDED IN THE YEAR 1824 THE ROYAL NATIONAL LIFE-BOAT INSTITUTION
AND IN 1832 BUILT THE TOWER OF REFUGE IN DOUGLAS BAY.
FEARLESS HIMSELF IN THE WORK OF RESCUE FROM SHIPWRECK HE HELPED TO SAVE 509 LIVES
AND WAS THREE TIMES AWARDED THE GOLD MEDAL OF THE INSTITUTION FOR GREAT GALLANTRY.
WHAT HIS WISDOM PLANNED AND POWER ENFORCED
MORE POTENT STILL HIS GREAT EXAMPLE SHOWED.
THOMSON

not swim, but he succeeded in clambering aboard the lifeboat and continued to play his part in the rescue.

In 1823 Hillary published in Douglas a pamphlet entitled *An Appeal to the British Nation on the Humanity and Policy of forming a National Institution for the Preservation of Lives and Property from Shipwreck.* The pamphlet came to the attention of Thomas Wilson, Member of Parliament for the City of London, and largely through Wilson's efforts a meeting was held at the City of London Tavern on 4th March 1824.

The chair was taken by the Archbishop of Canterbury, Dr Charles Manners Sutton, and among the resolutions passed was one calling for an organization to be brought into being named the National Institution for the Preservation of Life from Shipwreck. Eight months later, in November 1824, two similar bodies were established in the Netherlands to provide rescue services off the Dutch coast.

The organization founded at the meeting in the City of London Tavern came to be popularly, and rather unhappily, known as the Shipwreck Institution, and in 1854 its name was changed to Royal National Lifeboat Institution, commonly abbreviated as RNLI. The history of the RNLI over a period of more than 150 years has been largely that of the manner in which the blueprint which Hillary, with extraordinary prescience and care, offered in his pamphlet in 1823 has been adopted and adapted by his successors.

Volunteers in action

On the evening of Thursday 12th January 1899 a telegraph message was received at Lynmouth in North Devon that a ship was in distress in Porlock Bay and was in immediate danger of running ashore. Seas were sweeping across Lynmouth harbour and over the seafront, and after some discussion it was agreed that the Lynmouth lifeboat could not be launched.

Lynmouth and Porlock are separated by Countisbury Hill with a gradient of one in four and a half, a long stretch of open moor and then Porlock Hill, where the descent is in places almost sheer. The coxswain of the Lynmouth lifeboat suggested to the local vicar, who was also honorary secretary of the lifeboat station, that an attempt should be made to transport the lifeboat overland to Porlock. The vicar agreed.

The people of Lynmouth turned out in large numbers. Horses were produced from various quarters, one farmer from Lynton providing more than a dozen. The lifeboat signalman was sent ahead in charge of a small party equipped with pick-axes and shovels to widen the road where necessary. Flat wooden skids were taken by cart. Such light as there was came from flares and oil lanterns. A full gale was blowing from the west-north-west.

With the horses pulling and people pushing, the lifeboat on her carriage was slowly brought to the top of Countisbury Hill. A wheel then came off the carriage. This was put on again and a spare linchpin was fitted. On the most exposed part of Exmoor the road was found to be too narrow for the lifeboat to pass through on her carriage. The lifeboat was therefore dragged along on skids, and after some gateposts had been broken down the carriage was taken over the open moor to rejoin the lifeboat farther along the road.

In the descent down Porlock Hill the greatest danger was that the lifeboat would slip off her carriage. With the use of drag-ropes and safety chains this danger was averted, but near the bottom of the hill the road was again found to be too narrow for the lifeboat and carriage. To bring them through it was necessary to knock down a stone wall. It was agreed that this must be done.

An old woman living in a nearby cottage came out and asked indignantly what was happening. She had never before seen a lifeboat, but when it was explained to her why men were demolishing a wall in the middle of the night she joined enthusiastically in the work.

After a ten-and-a-half hour overland journey, without even stopping to eat, the Lynmouth crew put out in their lifeboat from Porlock and successfully escorted the 1900-ton full-rigged ship *Forrest Hall* to Barry in South Wales.

A similar overland journey conducted by horses and men took place between Whitby and Robin Hood's Bay in January 1881, with snow and ice adding to the hazards. Indeed before tractors, motorized lifeboats and radio communication were available journeys of this kind, though rarely needed, were accepted as part of the lifeboat service.

When they occurred the involvement of virtually the whole local community with the lifeboat, the lifeboat crew and the purposes they served became apparent. Yet at all times this involvement remained, as it remains today, latent at least in many coastal towns and villages. It is one of the reasons why the lifeboat service continues to be a voluntary one.

In the pamphlet which he published in Douglas in 1823, Hillary proposed that the organization needed to provide a comprehensive lifeboat service should be financed by voluntary donations and subscriptions. Obtaining these would, he thought, be 'found easy in its progress and successful in its results'.

He advocated this method of financing the RNLI, not from any disinclination to obtaining money from the Government, but because he believed it was the only method with a chance of succeeding. In this he was right. Eighteen years after the Shipwreck Institution came into being he wrote to the Home Secretary, Lord John Russell, asking

The Cox family of Wells, all
fishermen and lifeboatmen:
(left to right) Alan
radio-operator/second
mechanic, David coxswain,
Jack retired.

for help from public funds for the lifeboat
stations in the Isle of Man. Russell turned
the request down on the grounds that to give
such help would be 'a departure from the
general principle by which, in this country,
similar institutions are left to private
benevolence'.

In the first quarter of a century of its
existence the Shipwreck Institution did not
in fact achieve the successful results which
Hillary had confidently forecast, and its
record was unimpressive. There was an
encouraging start, with £10,000 being sub-
scribed in the Institution's first year, but in
its fifth year income barely exceeded £300.

There followed a period of inertia and,
it must be assumed, over-complacent
management. Between 1841 and 1850 no
public appeals were issued, and a number of
lifeboats became unserviceable through lack
of money and neglect. Yet the need for an
effective lifeboat service had never been
greater. In 1852 twenty ships on average
were wrecked each week round the coasts of
Britain and Ireland and eighteen lives lost
from shipwreck. The corresponding mod-

ern figures are about one-twentieth of those
of 1852.

Rescue for the body which was soon to be
named RNLI came in part from the choice
of the fourth Duke of Northumberland as a
new and inspiring president; in part by the
appointment of an exceptionally able secretary, a young barrister named Richard
Lewis; and not least from an annual grant
made by the Government, through the Mercantile Marine Fund, of £2000 per year.

This grant, though welcome when it was
first made, had unforeseen consequences,
which caused those responsible for adminis-
tering the RNLI's affairs to begin to wonder
whether the disadvantages of receiving
money from the Government might not
outweigh the advantages. As commonly
happens when Governments grant money,
conditions were imposed. One of these was
that a principal Coastguard officer or some
official of the Board of Trade should be a
member of the local committee of every
lifeboat station and that all applications for
payments should be countersigned by him.
Some of the local committees who were well

used to running their own stations with success found this form of control particularly irksome.

The grant from the Mercantile Marine Fund was first made in 1854. Before the end of 1869 the RNLI's Committee of Management felt able to dispense with the grant and asked for it to be discontinued. This was done.

The assumption underlying this decision was that the RNLI's finances were again in a healthy condition. To a limited extent this was true, but the basis of public support was still socially a very narrow one. This became apparent in the late 1880s, when there was a sudden upsurge of public interest in the conduct of the affairs of the RNLI. This followed, as so often happens, a major lifeboat disaster.

On 9th December 1886 the barque *Mexico* of Hamburg went aground near Southport in Lancashire. Three lifeboats, those stationed at Southport, at St Anne's and at Lytham, put out. The Southport and St Anne's lifeboats were both capsized with the loss of all but two men. The Lytham lifeboat rescued the twelve men who formed the crew of the barque.

The chairman of the St Anne's lifeboat committee at the time was a leading figure in the Lancashire cotton industry named Charles Macara. With the help of the press he launched a major appeal for support of the RNLI. He also made a careful examination of the RNLI's finances. From this it emerged that some two-thirds of the RNLI's regular income was provided by about a hundred people. This, Macara decided, would have to be changed.

Macara does not seem to have been found

Lifeboat street collection in Manchester in the 1890s.

an easy colleague by those concerned with the administration of the RNLI. He was probably both abrasive and dictatorial, but he was certainly effective. After enlisting the support of the mayors of Manchester and Salford he organized the first street-collection in October 1891. A procession included three bands and two lifeboats, which were later launched into an artificial lake. Money was thrown into collecting carts from upstairs windows and the tops of trams. The crowd which watched the final demonstration of a rescue by rocket apparatus was estimated at 30,000.

In the street-collections arranged by Macara in Manchester and Salford are found the origins of the flag day, which soon became a regular part of British life. Macara also provided the blueprint for fund-raising through the division of the country into dis-

tricts, and it was through his efforts more than those of any other individual that the RNLI was transformed from a cause supported by a limited number of the nobility and gentry into a major national charity, conducted by new methods and offering a new kind of popular appeal.

Criticism of the RNLI was not silenced by Macara's successes. Indeed the very flamboyance of his methods gave rise to charges of needless extravagance. In response to these and other complaints the House of Commons agreed to the appointment on 17th March 1897 of a select committee 'to enquire into the Administration of the Royal National Lifeboat Institution, and into the adequacy of its organization for Saving Life on our Coasts'. The committee's report, which was published in July, was a total vindication of

Ladies of the Dublin committee of the Saturday Lifeboat Fund, 1901.

following pages
Lifeboat Saturday in Brighton in 1899. The Lifeboat Saturday movement, which Sir Charles Macara initiated, brought pageantry to towns and villages and funds and publicity for the RNLI. Of Macara it was said: 'he brought charity into the streets and the streets into charity'.

Blackpool coxswain, Henry Parr, inspires future lifeboat supporters.

Fishwives in Cullercoats, Northumberland, were traditionally among the most determined RNLI collectors. Polly Donkin, seen here in 1933 aged 76, had in the preceding twelve years regularly made her rounds through the Derwent valley, collecting more than £500 for the RNLI.

the RNLI and the methods by which it was financed.

The RNLI's cause was certainly helped by the fact that its most vocal critic at the time was a man whose motives were thoroughly disreputable. This was the head of a carriage-building business named E. H. Bayley, whose products had been rejected by the RNLI on grounds of bad workmanship and whose subsequent attempt to bribe an RNLI employee to accept them had been exposed. Many witnesses were however heard, and the verdict of the committee was emphatic. 'Your committee,' the report stated, 'see no ground for recommending that the Lifeboat Service should be taken over by the State, so long as it is maintained as efficiently and successfully as at present by public benevolence.'

It was a verdict which society as a whole has subsequently accepted. During the two world wars of the twentieth century, when Governments could exercise almost total control over peoples' lives and property and heavy extra demands were made on the lifeboat service, the voluntary status of the RNLI was maintained. Indeed only in Ireland has there been any instance of State financing.

In spite of the establishment, first of the Irish Free State, and later of the Irish Republic, no separation of the lifeboat service has ever occurred. In consequence the RNLI is responsible for lifeboat stations in all parts of Ireland, south as well as north. In practice voluntary contributions in the Irish Republic fall short of the cost of maintaining the service there, and a hidden subsidy is in effect received from British donors. In recognition of this the Irish Government began in 1970 to make a small annual grant towards the cost of the lifeboat service in Ireland. This may be thought a reasonable compromise in what may also be thought both a satisfactory and an anomalous state of affairs.

Since 1919, when Edward Prince of Wales, later King Edward VIII, succeeded the Seventh Duke of Northumberland, the President of the RNLI has always been a member of the royal family. Edward Prince of Wales is seen here with a collector on London Lifeboat Day, 1926.

Income

In 1981 the RNLI needs at least £14½ million a year. A new Arun class lifeboat costs £350,000, an Atlantic 21 class costs £18,000 and an inflatable 16 ft boat £3,300. All the RNLI's funds derive from voluntary contributions.

Almost half the RNLI's income comes from legacies; special gifts from societies and commercial organizations, such as the Civil Service and the Post Office Lifeboat Fund and British Petroleum, have funded lifeboats. About 35% stems from local fund-raising activities. There are 14 fund-raising districts in the RNLI, each with a paid secretary and small staff who assist the fund-raising activities of over 2000 voluntary branches throughout the country. These range from the traditional flag day to a variety of events such as raffles and sponsored activities. The money raised by the branches is allocated by the RNLI headquarters, but many branches have a special association with particular lifeboat stations. The RNLI also runs a trading company dealing with souvenirs and gifts. There is a membership scheme, 'Shoreline', to enable people to support the RNLI by annual contributions.

Of every £1 contributed to the RNLI, 76 pence is spent directly on maintaining the fleet, building new boats and purchasing new equipment or shore facilities. Of the remainder, 16 pence goes on fund-raising and publicity, and 8 pence on administration.

Other than the few fulltime salaried crew members, lifeboatmen are volunteers. To compensate for loss of earnings while they are on service, they are paid £3 for the first hour of each call, and £1 for each hour thereafter.

In the 1960s it became increasingly apparent that, whereas more and more calls were being made on lifeboats to go to the help of pleasure craft, the RNLI's machinery for obtaining financial support from the owners of such craft was inadequate. A new membership scheme was therefore instituted early in 1969 known as the Yachtsmen's Lifeboat Supporters Association. Its first member and the official launcher of the scheme was Sir Alec Rose, who had recently returned from his single-handed voyage round the world. Out of this grew a general membership scheme known as Shoreline, whose funds provided a new lifeboat stationed at Blyth, Northumberland, in 1979. Sir Alec Rose is seen here at the Blyth lifeboat naming ceremony.

top left
RNLI collector trained by the mechanic of the Weymouth lifeboat.

top centre
Sue Punch of Shoreham, Sussex, who successfully bet that she would complete a week's work on a construction site; the money she raised by sponsorship was donated to the RNLI.

top right
The RNLI Appeals Secretary, Commander Ted Pritchard, a former Fleet Air Arm pilot, showered with money raised for the RNLI aboard the aircraft carrier HMS *Eagle*.

left
Lawn-mower racing during a 'yokels' fair' organized by customers of the Black Horse, Byworth, Sussex, in aid of the RNLI.

above and right
Many stage, film and television stars support RNLI fund-raising events. Harry Secombe visits Atlantic College in South Wales. Eric Morecambe at the International Boat Show in London with an outstandingly successful RNLI collector, Chelsea Pensioner Sergeant Frank Elverson.

opposite top
The Southsea Lifeboat, painting by W. L. Wyllie.

opposite bottom
The rescue by the Cromer lifeboat from the Italian steamer *Monte Nevoso* in 1932. In the pamphlet in which he advocated the formation of a lifeboat service in 1823, Sir William Hillary stated that lifeboats should go to the help of people and vessels of all nations both in peace and war. This principle has been accepted by the lifeboat services of the world.

following pages
Lifeboat attending wreck at the mouth of the Tyne 1837, painting by Stuart Henry Bell.

There are many advantages in the voluntary system. They include freedom from Government control, greater freedom to experiment and freedom from arbitrary budgetary cuts. The marked preference for the voluntary system shown by those engaged in the service and therefore, presumably, best qualified to judge must too be significant. But perhaps the most important consideration of all is the effect the voluntary system has on the nature and composition of crews and committees.

One almost certain consequence of state control of the lifeboat service would be the institution before long of full-time crews with a clause in their contracts stating that they could, if thought necessary, be transferred to other stations. Whether such crews would be more or less effective than those who man the boats at present must be a matter for speculation. But it is difficult to believe that the same intense local pride and the same satisfaction in local autonomy, which draw so many people of ability and dedication to work voluntarily for the lifeboat service, would be retained.

opposite
Coxwain Frank Ide of Poole,
at the wheel of a Waveney
lifeboat.

The Duke of Kent, President
of the RNLI, talking to
members of the Wells Ladies'
Lifeboat Guild.

Celebration of Queen
Victoria's Diamond Jubilee in
Plymouth. The crew of the
Penlee lifeboat in lifejackets,
the *Western Morning News* fire
brigade and collectors for the
RNLI.

At the Galway Bay station off the west coast of Ireland the honorary secretary has traditionally been the parish priest. The incumbent in 1952 is seen here with a visiting priest and the lifeboat crew.

A Northern Irish lifeboat crew. On 31st January 1953 the greatest disaster suffered by a British merchant vessel in time of peace for a quarter of a century occurred when the motor ship *Princess Victoria*, owned by the British Transport Commission, sank after leaving Stranraer for Larne with the loss of 133 lives. The Donaghadee lifeboat saved 31 people. Her crew, seen here, is one with a very strong family tradition. Many of them over the years have been named Nelson. The coxswain in 1953 was Hugh Nelson (front centre).

The quality of this pride was once succinctly expressed by a man of seventy-eight, who had been second coxswain of the lifeboat at Caister in Norfolk. His name was James Haylett. At the inquest into the loss of life following a capsize in 1901 the suggestion was put to him that the Caister lifeboat might have been returning after failing to accomplish her mission. In words which almost instantly became famous in more than one continent James Haylett replied: 'Caister men never turn back.'

There is no RNLI lifeboat station today at Caister, but there is a pub whose name must puzzle a number of visitors. It is called the Never Turn Back.

Wells:
portrait of a lifeboat station 1979

1 Coxswain David Cox
2 Second Coxswain Anthony Jordan
3 Oakley lifeboat crew
4 Lt David Case RNVR,
   station honorary secretary
5 Mrs David Case
6 Lt S. C. Long RNVR, deputy launching
   authority
7 Mr M. J. Hill, station honorary treasurer
8 Rev. David Chapman, chaplain
9 Dr D. W. Hoddy, honorary medical
   adviser
10 Lord Coke, president and patron
11 Branch committee representatives
12 HM Coastguards and Auxiliary
   Coastguards

13 Inflatable-lifeboat crew
14 Police
15 Shipwrecked Mariners' Society
16 Life guards
17 Launching crew
18 Brian Scoles, head launcher
19 Richard Woodgett, maroon firer
20 Ladies' guild committee members
21 Ladies' guild members
22 George Read, tractor driver

Wells lifeboat: a dawn search

The sequence of pictures on the following pages recalls a long and fruitless search by the Wells lifeboat one early morning in June 1977. Though undramatic, this incident is typical of the time-consuming, tedious and often unpleasant work regularly undertaken by RNLI crews throughout the year.

Preparing to launch, just before dawn . . .

Wells lifeboat: a dawn search

right
The launch, as dawn begins to break.

below
Crewman Graham Walker lights the last dry cigarette in gale-force winds.

opposite
Waiting, Ruby Cox, wife of Coxswain David Cox . . .

Wells lifeboat: a dawn search

right and below
The launchers prepare for the return of the lifeboat.

opposite top
The tractor's powerful winch pulls the lifeboat out of the water over the skids.

opposite bottom
The launchers balance the boat so that she can be hauled back on to her carriage.

36

Oars and sail

The history of the design and construction of lifeboats is one of a continual search for perfection diverted by a repeated need to compromise. It may even be argued that a lifeboat must be a form of compromise because of its very purpose.

A relatively small boat with a shallow draught is needed, yet it must be able to put out to the rescue when other vessels are seeking the shelter of harbour and do so with the minimum danger of capsize. Many forms of life-saving equipment can be useful on occasions, but only those may be carried which considerations of weight and space permit. A balance has to be struck between speed and sea-keeping qualities.

For the first hundred years of lifeboat construction the only forms of propulsion available were oars and sail, and the early designers often had to seek a compromise between the relative advantages of the two. Greathead's boat, the *Original*, was designed as a rowing boat. She was thirty

feet in length, and there were six pairs of oars. She rose sharply at both bow and stern, and for increased buoyancy she had cork-filled cases, cork lining and casing of cork along the gunwale.

By contrast boats designed specifically for the east coast of England, and known as the Norfolk and Suffolk type, were heavily built with almost flat bottoms. They were particularly well suited to operate in the heavy waters which can suddenly be whipped up by gales in the comparatively shallow North Sea. Only the smallest boats of this type could be effectively managed under oars alone, and the Norfolk and Suffolk boats were therefore essentially sailing lifeboats.

Nevertheless perfection continued to be sought, and soon after his appointment as President of the RNLI in 1851 the fourth Duke of Northumberland offered a prize for the best model of a lifeboat. By awarding points for particular qualities the adjudicating committee gave an indication of what in

The *Zetland*, the oldest surviving lifeboat, was stationed at Redcar. This private lifeboat, not in the service of the RNLI, was designed by Henry Greathead and built in 1800. She served for eighty years and is still preserved by the local council.

Illustrated London News artist's impression of how a pulling lifeboat put out to a wreck in Mount's Bay, Cornwall, in December 1868. The lifeboat, which was stationed at Penzance, was named *Richard Lewis* as a tribute to the first truly successful Secretary of the RNLI.

their opinion would constitute perfection. The committee's list of qualities demanded and possible points awarded was:

Qualities as a rowing boat in all weathers	20
Qualities as a sailing boat	18
Qualities as a sea-boat; as, stability, safety, buoyancy forward for launching through a surf	10
Small internal capacity for water up to level of thwarts	9
Means of freeing boat of water readily	8
Extra buoyancy; its nature, amount, distribution, and mode of application	7
Power of self-righting	6
Suitableness for beaching	4
Room for, and power of, carrying passengers	3
Moderate rate of transport along shore	3
Protection from injury of bottom	3
Ballast as iron (1), water (2), cork (3)	3
Access to stem or stern	3
Timber heads for securing warps to	2
Fenders, life-lines etc.	1
	100

The highest number of points the committee felt able to award for any one model was 84. The man who earned this number, and therefore the first prize, was a Yarmouth boat-builder named James Beeching, but the committee were not wholly satisfied and asked one of their own members, James Peake, the Assistant Master Shipwright at HM Dockyard, Woolwich, to modify Beeching's design in at least one important respect. Cork was fitted along the bottom in place of air chambers, and there was no water ballast.

The crews of the pulling and sailing lifeboats had few navigational or life-saving aids. Ropes, anchors, including the important sea anchor or drogue, a heaving line and grapnel and a compass made up the bulk of the equipment. The clothing worn provided only limited protection against the cold and the sea.

No more vivid description of how it felt to serve in a lifeboat before mechanical power was introduced has ever been given than that which appeared in the *Daily Telegraph* in January 1881. The writer was Clark Russell, a novelist of repute in his day who seems to be little read now. The rescue he described was from the 1238-ton ship *Indian Chief*, which went aground on the Long Sand, off the coast of Kent. The story was told largely in the words of the coxswain of the Ramsgate lifeboat, an impressive, bearded figure named Charles Fish.

'Our boat,' the coxswain told Russell, 'is

When a competition was staged in 1851 for the best design of a lifeboat there were 280 entries. Some were decidedly bizarre, including one which was described by the designer as being of 'whimsical construction' and which (like a lifebelt) was open to the sea at the bottom. Another built of wickerwork and covered with canvas could, it was claimed, be rolled along the beach and opened out at the scene of the disaster. Yet among the unorthodox entries was one with a real application for life-saving. This was the tubular lifeboat designed by two ingenious but slightly eccentric Welsh army officers named Richardson, who were father and son. Their boat consisted largely of two iron tubes, which were 40 feet in length. These were divided into watertight compartments, and their ends curved in to meet at head and stern. A platform, with rope network around it, was placed on the tube. From this the crew rowed the boat. The RNLI's first tubular lifeboat was stationed at Rhyl in 1856. Another, shown here, was in service at New Brighton from 1863 to 1898 and carried out a number of successful rescues.

considered a very fine one. I know there is no better on the coasts, and there are only two in Great Britain bigger. But it is ridiculous to talk of bigness when it means only forty-two feet long, and when a sea is raging round you heavy enough to swamp a line-of-battle ship.'

To enable her to reach the wreck quicker the lifeboat was towed out of Ramsgate harbour by the steam tug *Vulcan*. 'Things were not over and above comfortable,' Coxswain Fish said. 'We got out the sail-cover – a piece of tarpaulin – to make a shelter of, and rigged it up against the mast; but it hadn't been

up two minutes when a heavy sea hit and washed it right aft in rags; so there was nothing to do but to hold on to the thwarts and shake ourselves when the water came over. I never remember a colder wind. The feel of it in the face was like being gnawed by a dog. I only wonder it didn't freeze the tears it fetched out of our eyes.'

Information was sought from vessels encountered, including a collier and a smack. After a time, as the coxswain put it, 'The cold and the wet and the fearful plunging were beginning to tell, and one of the men called for a nip of rum. The quantity we generally take is half a gallon, and it is always my rule to be sparing with that drink for the sake of the shipwrecked men we may have to bring home, and who are pretty sure to be in greater need of the stuff than us. I never drink myself, sir, and that's one reason, I think, why I manage to meet the cold and wet middling well, and rather better than some men who look stronger than me.'

The lifeboat, still under tow, came up alongside the Kentish Knock lightvessel. 'She is a big, red-hulled boat,' Coxswain Fish said, 'with white letters on her sides, and, dark as it was, we could see her flung up, and rushing down fit to roll her over and over; and the way she pitched and went out of sight, and then ran up on the black heights of water, gave me a better notion of the

opposite bottom
The lifeboat stationed at Brighstone Grange in the Isle of Wight in the 1860s. The top-hatted figure on the left was the honorary secretary of the station, a clergyman named McCall. He is talking to the coxswain, whose name was Buckett and who is seated on the shaft. The tall, bearded figure (right centre) was the Secretary of the Isle of Wight Lifeboat Board.

above
Before steel and, later, glass-reinforced plastic construction was adopted lifeboats were traditionally built of a variety of woods, including English oak, African mahogany, Burmese teak and Western red cedar. Planing, sawing, fitting and chiselling called for exquisite craftsmanship. The scene here is a timber yard at Cowes in the Isle of Wight.

left
Coxswain Charles Fish of Ramsgate.

41

The lifeboat *Bradford* at the wreck of the *Indian Chief*.

fearfulness of that sea than I had got by watching the tug or noticing our own lively dancing.'

In the darkness there was no sign of the wreck, and the crews of the lifeboat and tug decided to lie-to all night. Charles Fish disclaimed any personal credit for this decision but stated: 'I am bound to say a word for the two crews, who made up their minds without a murmur, without a second's hesitation, to face the bitter cold and fierce seas of that long winter darkness, that they might be on the spot to help their fellow-creatures when the dawn broke and showed them where they were.'

The coxswain went on: 'We turned to and got the foresail aft, and made a kind of roof of it. This was no easy job, for the wind was so furious that wrestling even with that bit of a sail was like fighting with a steam-engine. We all lay in a lump together for warmth, and a fine show we made, I dare say; for a cork jacket, even when a man stands upright, isn't calculated to improve his figure, and as we all had cork jackets on and oil-skins, and many of us sea-boots, you may guess what a raffle of arms and legs we showed, and what a rum heap of odds and ends we looked, as we sprawled in the bottom of the boat upon one another.'

When dawn came the *Indian Chief* was sighted. 'All about the wreck was the Sand, and the water on it was running in fury all sorts of ways, rushing up in tall columns of foam as high as a ship's mainyard, and thundering so loudly that, though we were to windward, we could hear it above the gale and the boiling of the seas around us.'

As the lifeboat closed the wreck the sight which met Charles Fish and his crew was as gruesome as any Coleridge's Ancient Mariner might have recalled. 'A fearful wreck she looked, with her mainmast and mizenmast gone, and her bulwarks washed away, and great lumps of timber and planking ripping out of her and going overboard with every pour of the seas. There was a horrible muddle of spars and torn canvas and rigging under her lee, but we could not guess what a fearful sight was there until our hawser having been made fast to the wreck, we had hauled the lifeboat close under her quarter. There looked to be a whole score of dead bodies knocking about among the spars.'

Dead bodies they were. 'Seventeen were drowned, and there they were, most of them, and the body of the captain lashed to the head of the mizenmast, so as to look as if he were leaning over it, his head stiff upright and his eyes watching us, and the stir of the seas made him appear to be struggling to get to us'.

Eleven men were rescued by Ramsgate

Lifeboat crew at Hythe in Kent with their self-righting pulling lifeboat shortly after returning from a service in 1891 to a Glasgow ship which was driven ashore. The lifeboat was named The 'Mayer de Rothschild' in accordance with the RNLI's regular practice of giving lifeboats the name of the donor.

lifeboat from the *Indian Chief*. In concluding his account the coxswain said to Clark Russell: 'I know in my heart, and say it without fear, that from the hour of leaving Ramsgate harbour to the moment when we sighted the wreck's mast, there was only one thought in all of us, and that was that the Almighty would give us the strength and direct us how to save the lives of the poor fellows to whose assistance we had been sent.'

Nearly a hundred years later Richard Evans, former coxswain of the Moelfre lifeboat in North Wales, and for a long time the only living man to have won the RNLI's gold medal for gallantry twice, was appointed, on his retirement from active service, a lecturer for the RNLI. When describing his most exacting rescue he habitually used almost the very words with which Coxswain Charles Fish had concluded his narrative.

The lifeboat at Torquay
inspired a limerick quoted in
the *Encyclopaedia Britannica* as
an example of the verse-form:

The lifeboat that's kept at Torquay
Is intended to float in the suay:
The crew and the coxswain
Are sturdy as oxswain,
And as smart and as brave as can buay.

44

Lifeboats with engines

The earliest mechanically propelled lifeboats were steamboats. Sir William Hillary had been far-sighted enough to publish *A Plan for the Construction of a Steam Life-boat* in 1824, yet the RNLI's first steamboat was completed only in 1890. This gap in time suggests an excessive reluctance to accept new ideas, particularly as evidence, which rescues such as that from the *Indian Chief* provided, was available of the value of steam tugs.

There were difficulties to be overcome in the design and construction of steam lifeboats. It was recognized that it would not be easy to combine the shallow draught of a true lifeboat with screw propellers which could be of practical use. In fact the RNLI's first steam lifeboat, which began service at Harwich, was driven by a form of jet propulsion. A powerful centrifugal pump sucked in water through an inlet in the bottom and discharged it through outlets either at the stem or stern, the boat being forced by reaction against the water in one direction or the other.

Steam lifeboats were costly to maintain, for they required four full-time skilled men: a chief engineer, an assistant engineer and two firemen. They were restricted in their use to stations where they could be kept afloat at all states of the tide. Nevertheless the record of the RNLI's first steam lifeboat, *Duke of Northumberland*, strengthens the belief that steam lifeboats could with advantage have been introduced earlier. During her thirty-three years of service, first at

Whitby pulling lifeboat putting out to the help of a fishing-boat. The pulling lifeboat remained in service at Whitby until 1957. The boathouse in which she was kept was then converted into a museum. The boat is today one of only two pulling lifeboats of the RNLI in their original condition. The other is in the Mariners Museum in Newport News, Virginia.

left and below
Steam lifeboat built in 1897 and stationed at New Brighton being inspected in the River Thames. Steam lifeboat built in the same year and stationed at Grimsby.

A steam tug towing the Lytham lifeboat out to the rescue, 1862. Before steam lifeboats were introduced it was common for steam tugs to tow pulling lifeboats from harbour to the vicinity of a wreck.

Harwich, Essex, then at Holyhead, Anglesey, and finally at New Brighton, Cheshire, she took part in the rescue of 295 people.

In fact only six steam lifeboats were built for the RNLI, for with the development of the internal combustion engine it became apparent that a new and more suitable method of propelling lifeboats mechanically would soon be available.

In accepting the use of petrol engines the RNLI's Committee of Management showed justifiable caution. The early engines were unreliable, and the coxswains of the first motor lifeboats were informed emphatically that 'the motor is an auxiliary to the sails, which latter are the principal motive power'.

New problems of design arose. The fitting of comparatively heavy engines could not be allowed to destroy the balance of a boat. Propellers had to be placed so that they would be protected from damage when the lifeboat was approaching a wreck or being launched down a slipway. There was also an added risk of fire. The RNLI took this so seriously that it began to take out insurance policies on its boats. This practice was abandoned when it was discovered that the total amount paid out in premiums over a number of years vastly exceeded the total of claims.

The first experimental petrol engine was fitted into an existing lifeboat in 1904. The first RNLI boat designed from the outset as a motor lifeboat was completed four years later. Yet it was not until 1936 that the smallest class of lifeboat was fitted with two engines of sufficient power and reliability and yet small enough to be accommodated in a boat 35 feet 6 inches in length. Only then could it be safely felt that sail could be dispensed with in all classes of lifeboat.

Mechanical power soon made it possible for rescues to be effected which would have been beyond the capacity of pulling or sailing lifeboats. This was vividly demonstrated early in World War I, when the hospital ship *Rohilla* went aground off Whitby in October 1914 and a major contribution to the rescue was made by a motor lifeboat which was brought from Tynemouth, forty-four miles away. Yet though efficiency was improved and men had no longer to pull on oars or hoist sails, conditions of service, for many years after the introduction of the motor lifeboat, were not necessarily much more comfortable than those experienced by the Ramsgate crew who put out to the help of the *Indian Chief*.

In the village of Ballycotton in County Cork the story is still for instance told, and without any unnecessary embellishments, of the events which took place near there in February 1936.

There had been several days of calm weather and frost when the wind began to blow from the south-east, the quarter most feared in Ballycotton. By Monday 9th February gales had been blowing for three days.

The coxswain of the lifeboat, Patrick Sliney, was a fisherman, a man of erect bearing, quiet and slow-speaking. Shortly before midnight on the Monday his fishing-boat parted her moorings. He spent much of the night trying to recover her and damaged his hand painfully in doing so.

The honorary secretary of the lifeboat station, Robert Mahony, was the village postmaster. His duties included operating the manual telephone exchange and delivering the letters himself. A small, lively man, Mahony had a great respect for Patrick Sliney and once said of him that he was 'as decent a man as ever stood in a pair of shoes'.

During the gales the telephone lines connecting Ballycotton with the outside world were blown down, but a message did reach Mahony at eight o'clock on the morning of Tuesday 10th February. It was brought by a man who had driven twelve miles to deliver it. The message was that the Daunt Rock lightvessel had broken from her moorings and was drifting towards Ballycotton.

Mahony consulted Patrick Sliney, and they decided not to fire the maroons which normally called out the lifeboat for fear of alarming too many of the people of the village. Instead the crew were summoned by word of mouth.

They all came from a small group of families, every member of the crew being named either Sliney or Walsh. Patrick Sliney's brother Tom was the boat's mechanic. His son William was the youngest member of the crew and was seasick throughout most of the events which followed.

When the people of Ballycotton saw the lifeboat put out to sea they could hardly believe the evidence of their senses. Spray from the sea was flying over the lantern of the lighthouse, which stands 196 feet above the water. No children went to school that day because of the danger from flying slates, and the parish priest, Father Thornhill, asked the congregation to 'pray for the crew of the Ballycotton lifeboat, which has gone out on an errand of mercy'.

Some six miles out from Ballycotton the

opposite top
Three lifeboats at Thurso. On 1st April 1909 a new type of flotilla left the London docks. It consisted of a sailing lifeboat to be stationed at Thurso, Caithness-shire, and two of the new motor lifeboats to be stationed at Stromness and Stronsay in Orkney. The voyage to Thurso lasted seventeen days with enthusiastic receptions at the ports of call.

opposite bottom
Cullercoats lifeboat with engine and sail built in 1936.

following pages
Surf motor lifeboat built in 1934 nearing completion. These boats were specifically designed for operating in shallow water and had a limited operational range.

Building motor lifeboats of wooden construction. All lifeboats are built in private boatyards, most of them in the south of England. The Isle of Wight has a long history of lifeboat construction. Tenders are invited on a competitive basis when new lifeboats are about to be built. In practice the number of yards which can satisfy the RNLIs exacting demands is limited. After some 25 years of operational service, lifeboats are sold on the open market and still command appreciable prices because of the quality of their hulls and general design.

John McNamara, one of the survivors of the crew of the Fethard (Co. Wexford) lifeboat, which capsized in February 1914 with the loss of nine men. He spent three days without food while stranded on a rock.

lifeboat met exceptionally heavy seas, and Patrick Sliney decided he must put out the canvas drogue to steady the boat. He eased the engines, and immediately several seas struck him on the side of the head and he was half stunned. Then, as the drogue was being put out, a heavy, curling sea came over the port quarter, filled the cockpit, and knocked down every man on board. When they recovered they found that the drogue-ropes had fouled, but the drogue was drawing.

The lifeboat searched the area where the lightvessel was normally stationed but could not find her, and Patrick Sliney decided to make for the harbour then known as Queenstown, now known as Cobh. There the position of the lightvessel was known, and the lifeboat put out again.

When the lifeboat reached the lightvessel she found two ships standing by, HM destroyer *Tenedos* and SS *Innisfallen*. The crew of the lightvessel were determined not to leave her, for she was a long way from her correct position and therefore a danger to navigation. They asked the lifeboat to stand by too.

For hours the lifeboat steamed and drifted. A line was secured to the lightvessel, but it quickly parted. Darkness came on, and it was agreed that the destroyer would stand by all night and that the lifeboat would put in briefly to Cobh. There the crew took on a spare drogue and drogue-rope and had a change of underclothing, which Mahony had brought by car.

Early on the morning of Wednesday 11th February the lifeboat put out again. She stood by the lightvessel all day. The weather forecast in the evening offered no hope of an improvement in the conditions, and Patrick Sliney suggested the time had come to take off the lightvessel's crew. The master would not agree and the lifeboat stood by all night.

When daylight came the lifeboat had little petrol left, and it was clear she would have to return once more to Cobh. Mahony had arranged for eighty gallons of petrol to be put on a lorry at Cork, but the driver in his eagerness to leave squeezed his arm in a gate and damaged it so badly that he could not drive. There was some delay before another driver could be found, and it was not until four o'clock in the afternoon that the lifeboat was able to put out again with the

55

The Ballycotton lifeboat crew that was involved in the epic rescue of the lightvessel crew in February 1936.

prospect of having to stand by through yet another night of gales.

The lifeboat reached the lightvessel at dusk. The lightvessel had drifted to within sixty yards of rocks, and Patrick Sliney pointed out that if the wind shifted farther to the west she would certainly strike them. So at last it was agreed that the lifeboat should try to take off the lightvessel's crew.

Seas were now sweeping right over the lightvessel. She was plunging on her cable, rolling from thirty to forty degrees and burying her starboard bow in the water. She was fitted with rolling chocks, which projected more than two feet from her sides, and as she rolled these threshed the water. Because of the lightvessel's cable it was impossible to anchor to windward and veer

down on her, and Patrick Sliney realized he could do nothing but approach her from astern and make quick runs in on her port side.

The lightvessel was only 98 feet long, and if the 51-foot lifeboat, coming in at full speed, ran too far, she would go over the cable and capsize. Every time she came alongside, the lightvessel, with her chocks threshing the water as she plunged and rolled, might easily crash on top of the lifeboat. All these dangers were clear to the coxswain as he made his plan.

He first went ahead of the lightvessel and pumped oil, but it had little effect in calming the sea. Then he went astern and drove at full speed alongside. One man jumped successfully, and the lifeboat went astern. The

56

second time she went in nobody jumped, and again she went astern. The third time five men jumped, leaving two men on the lightvessel. Then came the fourth attempt.

This time the lightvessel sheered violently and her counter crashed on top of the lifeboat, smashing the rails and damaging the fender and deck. Nobody was hurt, but the man working the lifeboat's searchlight sprang clear at the last second. The lifeboat then went in a fifth time, and nobody jumped.

The lifeboat's crew now saw what was happening. The two remaining men were clinging to the rails and seemed unable to jump. Patrick Sliney therefore had to expose some of his crew to a new danger. He sent them forward, knowing they might easily be swept overboard, with orders to seize the two men as the lifeboat came alongside. The orders were carried out, and the two men were seized and dragged into the lifeboat.

The lifeboat left the lightvessel, but the dangers to her crew were not over. One of the lightvessel's crew, overcome by the strain he had undergone, became hysterical. He wanted to jump overboard, and two lifeboatmen, themselves exhausted, had to hold him down by force.

When the lifeboat returned to Ballycotton in weather which had suddenly improved she had been away from her station for $76\frac{1}{2}$ hours and at sea for 49.

A 42-foot Watson lifeboat built in 1954 and stationed at Coverack, Cornwall. The fitting of a cabin in this small class of lifeboat was a new development.

Righting and non-righting boats

Self-righting trials in 1866, testing the self-righting capacity of the *City of Exeter* lifeboat. It has been the RNLI's regular practice to capsize every self-righting lifeboat during its trials to check its righting capacity.

To design a boat which is virtually unsinkable is not difficult. A floating object filled with a large number of table-tennis balls and divided into watertight compartments would probably continue to float in almost any circumstances. This principle was indeed adopted in the construction of many lifeboats. All the space below deck not required for machinery, fuel or survivors was filled with air cases, i.e. hollow wooden boxes covered with calico and moulded to the shape of the hull.

By contrast man has not yet succeeded in designing a small boat which can fulfil the

58

purposes of a lifeboat and which will not in certain circumstances capsize. Indeed it is the tacit assumption that lifeboats may, and sometimes will, capsize which has given rise to the controversy over the relative merits of self-righting and non-self-righting boats. This controversy has extended across some two centuries in time.

The model which William Wouldhave submitted to the Gentlemen of the Lawe House in 1789 was of a self-righting boat. His inspiration came from watching a woman taking water from a well with a curved wooden dipper. No matter how she inserted it the dipper always reverted to the upright position. By the time the committee members and Henry Greathead had com-

pleted their modifications the boat was no longer a self-righter. The self-righting quality had been sacrificed in the interests, it was believed, of greater stability. The boat's record of service may be thought to have justified the committee's decision.

The adjudicators of the 1851 competition indicated the importance they attached to the 'power of self-righting' by awarding it only six points out of a possible total of 100. Nevertheless the boat designed by Beeching and modified by Peake was a self-righter, and for some thirty-five years the prevailing belief within the RNLI was that a self-righting capability was a requisite feature of lifeboat design.

This belief does not seem to have been publicly questioned until after the disaster involving the Southport and St Anne's lifeboats in December 1886. The Southport lifeboat had capsized as the coxswain was about to let go an anchor and veer down on the German vessel in distress. What happened to the St Anne's boat was never fully established, for the whole crew were lost, but she was found bottom up with three dead bodies hanging on the thwarts with their heads downwards. It could therefore be assumed that the St Anne's boat failed to right herself, and the stability of both boats was called into question.

One consequence of the disaster was the appointment in 1887 of George Lennox Watson as the RNLI's Consulting Naval Architect. Watson was already a designer of international repute, and he was later to enjoy even greater fame as the designer of the royal yacht *Britannia* and of a number of contenders, albeit unsuccessful, for the America's Cup. Fifty years after Watson's appointment the RNLI journal stated that 'he more than any other man was the designer of the lifeboat fleet as it is today'. Lifeboats belonging to the so-called 'Watson' classes continued in the service of the RNLI for about a hundred years, some of them pulling or sailing boats, others driven by petrol or diesel engines.

When he appeared before the Select Committee of the House of Commons in 1897 Watson summarized his opinions on lifeboat design. It would, he said, be 'unwise and unsafe' to dispense with the self-righting quality in the smaller pulling boats, but he added: 'With the larger sailing boats I think we can get a better boat by abandoning the self-righting principle.'

This abandonment of the self-righting principle became standard practice during

the next half-century and was not confined to the larger boats. There was a tendency, which some of the designs seemed to justify, to equate self-righting with instability. Crews commonly described the small 35-foot 6-inch self-righting boats as 'roly-polies', and by 1957, out of a total RNLI active and reserve fleet of 178, the number of self-righters was no more than six.

Nevertheless disasters continued to occur, even to the more stable non-self-righters, and when they did, all or nearly all of the crew were normally lost. In Scotland the Fraserburgh lifeboat capsized in 1953 with the loss of six crew members out of seven; a year later the Arbroath lifeboat

capsized, also with six men lost out of seven. Within the RNLI the regularity of the disasters and the loss of life they caused were thought, reasonably enough, to justify a re-examination of the merits of self-righting lifeboats.

The outcome of this was the construction of a new kind of self-righter. Her designer,

Richard Oakley, had been an apprentice in the boat-building trade in the Isle of Wight, and had spent nearly all his working life in the service of the RNLI, being eventually appointed its Naval Architect. The first Oakley lifeboat, which was placed on service at Scarborough in 1958, was 37 feet in length with her self-righting capability

The Fraserburgh lifeboat after the capsize in 1953. This was one of the accidents which led to a re-examination of the merits of non-self-righting lifeboats.

achieved by an ingenious method of shifting water ballast. A ton-and-a-half of water was placed in a ballast tank. If the boat capsized the great bulk of the water was automatically transferred to a righting tank. This eased the boat to an angle where her reserve buoyancy brought her upright again.

The Oakley method was somewhat cumbersome in comparison with the principle of self-righting by virtue of shape which had inspired Wouldhave. The most important feature of the first Oakley boat was that she was shown, through exhaustive tank tests of models, to be an appreciably more stable boat than the non-self-righting boats of approximately the same size which she was expected to replace. This combination of stability and self-righting capacity was a clear advance in lifeboat design.

Following the success of the Oakley boats the RNLI rapidly introduced a number of other kinds of self-righting lifeboat into its fleet. The means by which they could be righted approximated more closely to the principle which inspired Wouldhave than to

the method adopted by Oakley. By 1970 it was accepted that virtually all lifeboats should have a self-righting capability, and the RNLI aimed to achieve this in about ten years. One of the most ambitious boat-building programmes in the RNLI's history was launched, and modifications were made to a number of existing boats. Some were largely rebuilt and so were converted into self-righters. Others were fitted with inflatable air-bags which, if a capsize occurred, could bring them upright once. The device, however, would not work if there was a second capsize.

The disaster off the Lancashire coast in December 1886 had been unique in that it had been the only occasion on which two lifeboats had capsized when going to the help of the same vessel. Not until 1979 was there a similar occurrence.

The casualty to which the lifeboats put out on this occasion was a Danish cargo vessel, *Lone Dania*, which shortly before midnight on 17th November was reported in distress near the Skerryvore lighthouse in

62

above
Richard Oakley, RNLI naval architect and designer of the Oakley self-righting lifeboat. His standing as a lifeboat designer was effectively confirmed when an Irish schoolgirl, taking part in an essay competition, wrote of lifeboats that they were constructed 'either of steel or of Oakley'.

left
Self-righting pulling lifeboat at Courtown in County Wexford, a station which was operational for only sixty years, from 1865 to 1925.

63

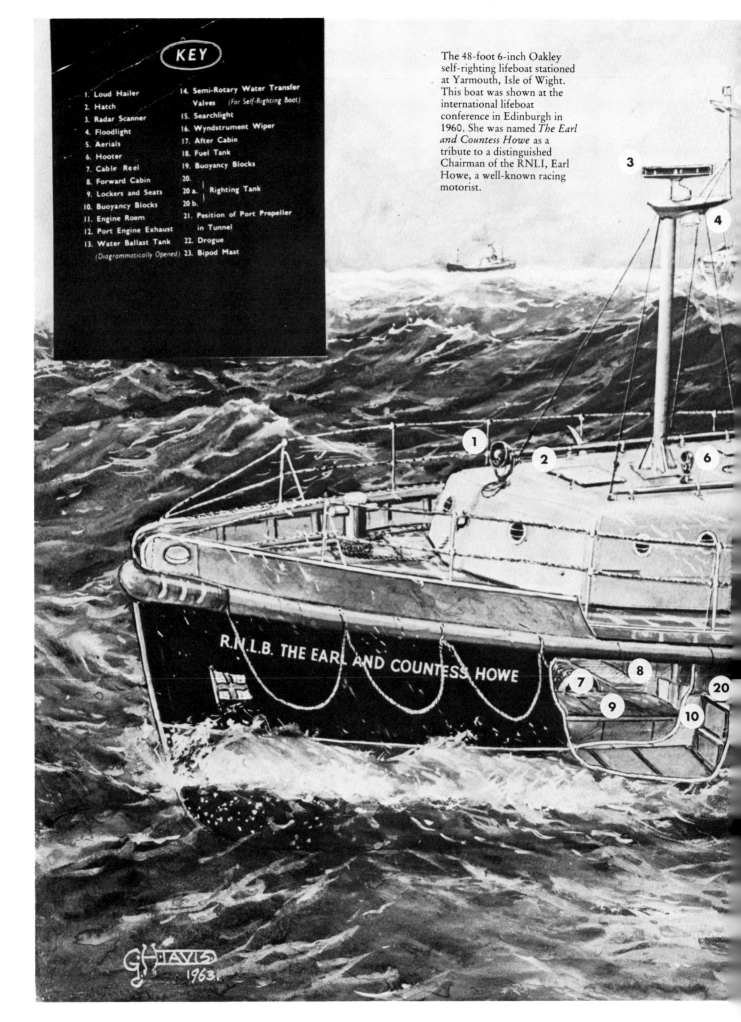

KEY

1. Loud Hailer
2. Hatch
3. Radar Scanner
4. Floodlight
5. Aerials
6. Hooter
7. Cable Reel
8. Forward Cabin
9. Lockers and Seats
10. Buoyancy Blocks
11. Engine Room
12. Port Engine Exhaust
13. Water Ballast Tank
    (Diagrammatically Opened)
14. Semi-Rotary Water Transfer
    Valves (For Self-Righting Boat)
15. Searchlight
16. Wyndstrument Wiper
17. After Cabin
18. Fuel Tank
19. Buoyancy Blocks
20.
20 a. } Righting Tank
20 b.
21. Position of Port Propeller
    in Tunnel
22. Drogue
23. Bipod Mast

The 48-foot 6-inch Oakley self-righting lifeboat stationed at Yarmouth, Isle of Wight. This boat was shown at the international lifeboat conference in Edinburgh in 1960. She was named *The Earl and Countess Howe* as a tribute to a distinguished Chairman of the RNLI, Earl Howe, a well-known racing motorist.

R.N.L.B. THE EARL AND COUNTESS HOWE

G. H. DAVIS 1963

CROSS SECTION OF 4846
PROTOTYPE LIFE BOAT
LOOKING AFT

Engine Room

motors

Righting
Tank

P.V.C.
Buoyancy
Blocks

Water
Ballast

Semi-rotary
Transfer
Valves

Two disasters within a year in Scottish waters caused the RNLI to undertake a greatly accelerated boat-building programme with the object of having a self-righting fleet by about 1980. The Longhope, Orkney, lifeboat, seen here being towed in, capsized with the loss of her whole crew of eight when going to the help of a Liberian vessel on 17th March 1969.

the Inner Hebrides. One of the lifeboats launched was of the 50-foot Thames class, a self-righter of steel construction stationed at Islay. The other, which was stationed at Barra Island, was of the Barnett class, 52 feet in length and built of wood. She was a non-self-righter and was fitted with an inflatable air-bag.

The wind, which was from the south-west, rose at times to hurricane force. The coxswain of the Barra Island lifeboat, John Macneil, who had been regularly at sea off the west coast of Scotland for seventeen

years as lifeboatman and merchant seaman, said afterwards that he had never known worse conditions. In the Islay lifeboat a member of the crew named Iain Spears, while bracing himself in a corner of the wheelhouse, landed heavily on one foot. Such was the force of the impact that it was discovered later that his ankle was broken.

A steep, breaking sea, some thirty feet high, appeared on the starboard bow of the Islay lifeboat. This sea was at right angles to the general run and may have rebounded off a reef. The lifeboat seemed first to hang there

The second disaster in Scottish waters. On 21st January 1970 the Fraserburgh lifeboat, with a crew of six, put out when a Danish fishing fleet was reported in distress. The lifeboat is seen here in the background, at the moment of capsize, caught by an enormous breaking wave. There was only one survivor.

Self-righting trials of Solent Class lifeboat, the immediate successor of the Oakley 48-foot 6-inch boat. This boat is of steel construction.

Atlantic 21 class lifeboat being tested at the RNLI base at Cowes. The boat is deliberately capsized with her crew on board and rights herself in seconds through the inflation of an air-bag. The electrical equipment and engines are made watertight so that the engines can be restarted at the push of a button.

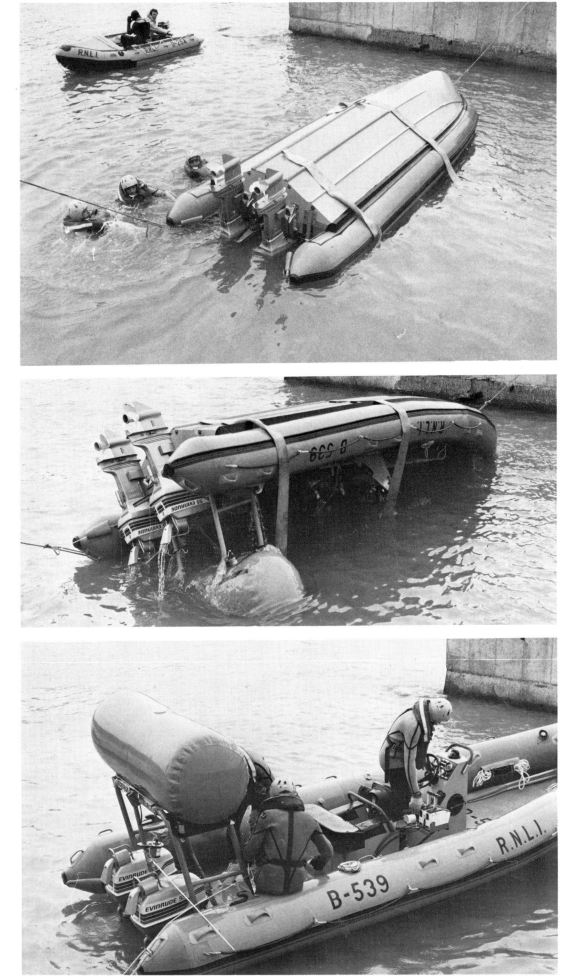

and then slide down the face of the approaching wave.

The wave broke aboard and capsized the lifeboat. She settled down for perhaps five seconds and then began to right herself. Afterwards members of the crew commented on the gentleness of the process of capsize and righting. One crew member was severely bruised, but the rest escaped lightly. The engines responded correctly and were found to be in gear but idling. The worst damage was to the radar and the windscreen wipers, both of which were put out of action.

Rather more than two hours later, that is to say shortly before four o'clock in the morning, Coxswain Macneil of Barra Island lowered a wheelhouse door window to see whether the Skerryvore light was visible. While his head was still out of the window the lifeboat seemed suddenly to pitch down by the bow and start rolling to port. The coxswain looked back and saw a breaking

sea some thirty to forty feet high towering over the lifeboat.

The lifeboat slewed violently to starboard, broached and rolled over to port. Water rushed into the wheelhouse and cabin. The boat continued her roll through 360 degrees, returning to the upright with the air-bag inflated.

Four of the Barra Island crew suffered head injuries, which were comparatively slight, but damage to the lifeboat was appreciable. The propellers had been fouled by the drogue, and it was almost impossible to clear them. Nevertheless a radio message was successfully sent to the Coastguard, and a coaster was diverted and took the lifeboat in tow. Another Danish coaster escorted the *Lone Dania* to Barra.

When the Southport and St Anne's lifeboats capsized in 1886 twenty-seven men were lost. The loss of life when the Islay and Barra Island lifeboats capsized in 1979 was nil.

below and following pages
Capsize of the Barra Island lifeboat while on service in November 1979. The air-bag, which inflated automatically to right the boat, is clearly visible in the stern. The pictures show the boat being towed back to harbour.

The search for speed

Speed has only recently been considered an important quality in a lifeboat. When a vessel goes aground on rocks or on a sandbank danger to life may not be immediate. In the traditional example of nineteenth-century rescue the lifeboat often succeeded in taking off the crew of a stranded vessel hours after the stranding took place. Sometimes the lifeboat was asked to stand by for more than one tide, and on such occasions it was of little consequence whether she first arrived on the scene an hour earlier or an hour later.

A requirement for speed began to be acknowledged within the RNLI when in the twentieth century it was confronted with a new kind of casualty. This was a direct consequence of the invention of the flying machine. When an aircraft crashes into the sea every minute gained in bringing a rescue vessel to the scene of the disaster is likely to be of importance. It was therefore logical that the first boat built for the RNLI which could achieve a speed of 18 knots should

have been intended largely for the rescue of survivors from aircraft which came down in the English Channel.

This boat, which was brought into service shortly before World War II, was stationed at Dover. Twin engines of 375 h.p. each made a speed of 17 or 18 knots possible, and she had a range of 78 miles at full power. She was the largest boat in the RNLI's service, being 64 feet in length. She was not expected to operate in the worst sea conditions, and her engines were not made watertight.

The high-speed Dover lifeboat was the first and last of her kind built for the RNLI. The Royal Air Force accepted responsibility for air-sea rescue, and the launches constructed for this purpose were a logical progression from the Dover boat.

After World War II another major change in the pattern of casualties gave rise to a new requirement for speed. This was a consequence of the enormous increase in the number of people who put to sea for their own pleasure in sailing boats, power boats,

RAF Sunderland flying-boat wrecked off Eastbourne in June 1955 with Eastbourne lifeboat standing by. Watched by hundreds of holiday-makers the flying-boat made what appeared to be a normal landing, then dipped its nose into the sea and began to sink. Ten men were taken off, a number of them seriously injured. Three men were lost.

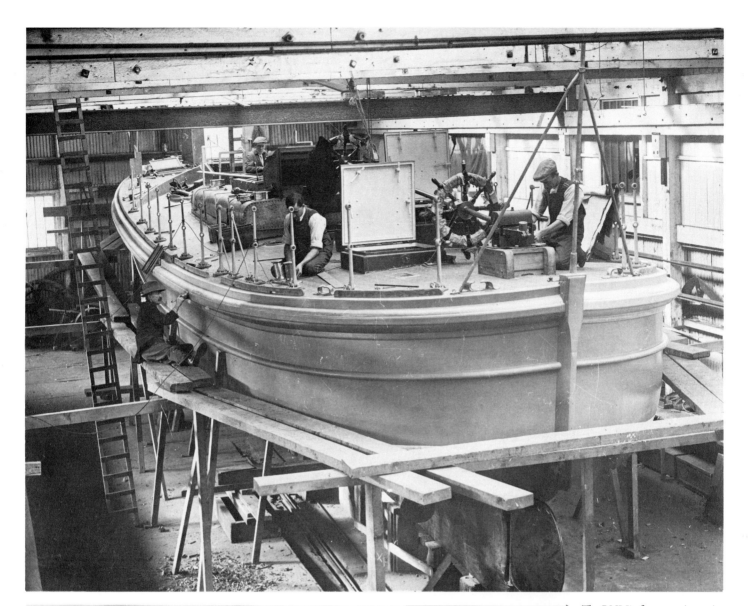

The RNLI's first experiment in building fast lifeboats. The 64-foot lifeboat completed in 1930, named *Sir William Hillary* and stationed at Dover: (above) under construction; (left) during her naming ceremony. Her speed was about 18 knots. This boat was both a novelty and the last of her kind to be built. Her natural successors were the fast rescue launches used by the RAF in World War II. When the RNLI began to build faster boats after the war, new designs and methods of construction were adopted.

canoes and other kinds of small and sometimes vulnerable craft.

In the first decade or more after 1945 the RNLI was, arguably, somewhat hesitant in adapting itself to new requirements. A belief in the excellence of the traditional RNLI lifeboats, which was not unreasonable, tended to mask a reluctance to take advantage of some of the new designs and developments which had been made possible by the exigencies of war and by the growth of a power-boat industry. The inspiration for the introduction by the RNLI after World War II of faster types of rescue boat came in fact from lifeboat organizations overseas.

A small, voluntary rescue service operating mainly in Brittany and known as the *Société des Hospitaliers Sauveteurs Bretons* seems to have led the world in the use for life-saving of small, fast, inflatable boats fitted with outboard engines. These were provided mainly for the benefit of holiday-makers at coastal resorts.

Within the RNLI there had been increasing awareness that lifeboats with a speed of 8 or 9 knots, some of them launched by the cumbersome method of carriage and tractor, were not the most suitable craft for rescuing people from dinghies which had capsized in a light wind and a slight sea. It was therefore decided to take advantage of the Breton experiment. In 1963 ten places were chosen at which inflatable boats would serve. The first boat to become operational was stationed at Aberystwyth in Dyfed.

The RNLI gave this new type of life-saving craft the cumbersome name 'inshore rescue boat'. At lifeboat stations they were generally known as 'rubber ducks'. They were 15 feet 6 inches in length, driven by a single outboard engine, built of neoprene-proofed nylon and fitted with five or six separate buoyancy compartments.

These boats were the first in the service of the RNLI to have a speed of more than 20 knots. They could be launched quickly. They needed a crew of no more than two or, at the most, three. Their cost, when they first came into commission, was less than £1000.

Two of the original inshore rescue boat

opposite
Small inflatable lifeboats, used for rescue work close inshore, are carried aboard certain of the larger classes of modern lifeboats. One is seen being launched from the Arun class lifeboat stationed at Torbay.

below
Atlantic 21 lifeboat airborne in trials at the Shingle Bank off the Isle of Wight.

An ingenious launching device
for Atlantic lifeboats developed
by the RNLI and operated at
Littlestone in Kent.

opposite top left
Coxswain Brian Bevan of the
Humber, the only man ever to
have received three RNLI
medals for gallantry at the
same annual meeting.

opposite top right
Launch of 48-foot 6-inch
Oakley class lifeboat at
Padstow, 1979.

opposite bottom
The Falmouth lifeboat
approaching the schooner
Mina, from which she rescued
ten people in August 1972.

following pages
An Atlantic 21 on trials off the
Isle of Wight.

stations were educational establishments, which were able and willing to provide crews from their staff and pupils. One was the Outward Bound School at Aberdovey. The other was the United World College of the Atlantic, usually known as Atlantic College, at St Donat's Castle in South Wales. Atlantic College was also the scene of important experiments in the development of fast rescue boats. They were conducted under the guidance of the college's headmaster, a rear-admiral, engineer and naval architect named Desmond Hoare.

The first inshore rescue boats, or inshore lifeboats, as they soon came to be called, were envisaged as rescue craft for the summer months. They were not designed to operate in the most severe conditions, at night, or more than a few miles from the shore. Indeed many of the inshore lifeboat stations were closed during the winter months. Nevertheless the first boats were, within their limitations, so successful that it was a logical progression to design, as Desmond Hoare did, a boat of similar type but with greater range and general capacity. This boat, which became known as the Atlantic, had two 50-h.p. outboard engines, which gave her a speed of 29 knots. Navigation lights enabled her to operate at night, and she had an endurance of over three hours at full speed.

With the steady growth in the number of

inshore lifeboat stations the RNLI found it expedient to establish a depot for the service and maintenance of the boats at Cowes in the Isle of Wight. Here too experiments were carried out, for the superintendent of the depot, David Stogdon, was, like Desmond Hoare, a man of inventive mind.

Stogdon, the son of a clergyman schoolmaster, received part of his education at Prague University. He served as an officer in the Royal Navy in World War II and subsequently as a lifeboat inspector. He had no formal training as a naval architect, yet was responsible for another major development in fast rescue boats. This was the Medina boat, the prototype of which was completed in 1979.

The Medina was envisaged as an intermediate lifeboat, bridging for the first time the considerable gap which still lay between the Atlantic and the conventional lifeboat which can be expected to operate in almost any conditions. She had a speed of 26 knots. Seventeen years before the Medina prototype was completed no boat in the service of the RNLI had a speed of more than 11.

The introduction and development of the fast rescue boat may be considered one of the greatest achievements in the RNLI's history. The official figures showed that by 1970 the number of people rescued by inshore lifeboats in one year (702) exceeded those rescued by the conventional boats

(555) for the first time. This trend continued.

In effect a new fleet had been brought into being to operate alongside the existing one. The challenge presented by the advent of large numbers of pleasure-boat sailors had been met with flexibility and a remarkable measure of success. In meeting it the RNLI had wisely enlisted the help of the pleasure-boat sailors themselves.

For many years lifeboat crews were formed almost exclusively from fishermen, pilots and others who regularly earned their living at sea. There had always been exceptions. Major-General J. E. B. Seely, later Lord Mottistone, who held the office of Secretary of State for War, was a member of the lifeboat crew at Brooke in the Isle of Wight for more than forty years and coxswain for three. In modern times William Morris, a long-serving coxswain, was the verger at St David's Cathedral, Dyfed. Other examples could be cited, but for a long time such people were noticeable because they were exceptional.

With the steady decline of the inshore fishing industry the number of fishermen in many of the lifeboat crews gradually dwindled, but there was still a reluctance to accept as a crew member any man whose knowledge of the sea was confined to pleasure-boat sailing. With the introduction of the inshore rescue boat this was changed. It was soon appreciated that the small, fast boats should be manned by the relatively young rather than the relatively old. Experience in power boats and sailing boats was deemed an advantage, and people of many occupations suddenly found themselves eligible and accepted for lifeboat service. The increase in the range of vessels from which rescues were effected had been accompanied by a corresponding increase in the range from which the rescuers were drawn.

In 1963, the year in which inshore lifeboats came into service, the ninth international lifeboat conference was held in Edinburgh. One paper aroused particular interest. It was presented by the United

opposite
About to pick up a survivor.

below
Inflatable lifeboat stationed at North Berwick and named *Blue Peter III*. The cost of many of the RNLI's lifeboats has been met by individuals, either through their wills or in their lifetime. Others have been provided by group efforts. In addition to the Civil Service and Post Office Lifeboat Fund the RNLI has received gifts of lifeboats from Scouts, Freemasons, Rotarians, Round Tablers, Foresters and Oddfellows. Funds to provide lifeboats for the RNLI have been raised by citizens of the USA and Southern Africa. Among commercial firms which have provided lifeboats have been *The Boys' Own Paper* and Birds Eye Foods. Four inflatable lifeboats were provided by viewers of the BBC television programme Blue Peter, who in December 1966 began collecting paperback books to raise funds.

right and opposite top
Intermediate lifeboats
developed in the late 1970s.
Both are prototypes. The
Medina (right), 40 feet in
length, has a speed of 26 knots.
The Brede (opposite) is an
adaptation of a commercial
craft; she is 33 feet in length
with a speed of 20 knots.

opposite bottom
Waveney class lifeboat
formerly stationed at Dover on
exercise.

States Coast Guard and described a new kind of lifeboat of steel and aluminium construction. The boat was 44 feet in length and was a self-righter. She had excellent sea-keeping qualities and remarkable manoeuvrability, as a film which was shown at the conference indicated. Significantly her speed was 14 knots. To a number of delegates to the conference the US Coast Guard paper seemed a pointer to the lifeboat of the future.

The RNLI bought one of the new 44-foot boats from the US Coast Guard and subjected her to extensive and intensive trials round the coasts of Britain and Ireland. In command was a long-serving staff coxswain, Sid Hills, who, when he retired, had almost certainly spent more hours at sea in RNLI lifeboats than any other man alive. Many RNLI coxswains were asked to take the wheel during the trials, and a certain initial scepticism, which derived not least from the evident contrast in appearance between this

boat and traditional RNLI lifeboats, was usually quickly dissipated.

Acting on the evidence of the trials the RNLI decided to build its own 44-foot lifeboats to designs which were freely provided by the US Coast Guard. The first boats were built at Lowestoft and given the class name Waveney, for the RNLI had by then begun to give new classes of lifeboat the names of the rivers on which the first of them were built. Had the older and perhaps happier practice of applying the name of the designer been retained, the class-name would probably have been Witter. This would have appropriately commemorated the important contribution made by a United States Coast Guard, Robert Witter.

The Waveney lifeboats had one major limitation. They could not be launched down slipways or from beaches, and their use was therefore confined to lifeboat stations with deep-water harbours. So far as the general coverage provided by the RNLI

Waveney lifeboat.

44 FT. STEEL LIFEBOAT. MK II.

LENGTH O.A.	44'-0"
LENGTH W.L.	40'-0"
BEAM O.A.	12'-1"
DRAFT	3'-7"

1. FAIRLEAD.
2. BOLLARD.
3. EMERGENCY TILLER CAP.
4. STEERING GEAR.
5. LOCKER SEAT.
6. STERN FLOODLIGHT.
7. GRAB RAIL.
8. STOKES STRETCHER.
9. MAIN ENGINES.
10. 5 GALLON FOAM CANS.
11. QUICK ACTING W.T. DOORS.
12. EXHAUST OUTLET.
13. ENGINE EXHAUST SILENCER.
14. TOWING BOLLARD.
15. BREECHES BUOY.
16. STEERING TRANSMISSION.
17. CONSOLE.
18. COMPASS.
19. RADAR DISPLAY UNIT.
20. HELMSMAN'S SEAT.

21. ENGINE ROOM VENTILATION TRUNKING.
22. SHIP'S BELL.
23. STERN LIGHT.
24. SEARCHLIGHT.
25. TOWING LIGHT.
26. U.H.F. DIPOLE AERIAL.
27. MASTHEAD LIGHT.
28. RADAR SCANNER.
29. STRAIGHT LINE WINDSCREEN WIPER.
30. 60 LB. DANFORTH ANCHOR.
31. CHEMICAL TOILET.
32. RADIO TELEPHONES.
33. LIFTING EYEPLATE.
34. WHIP AERIAL.
35. BOAT HOOK.
36. W.T. HATCH.
37. ECHO SOUNDER.
38. HYDRAULIC WINDLASS.
39. STEMHEAD FAIRLEAD & JACK STAFF SOCKET.
40. ANCHOR LIGHT.

GREENFIELD.

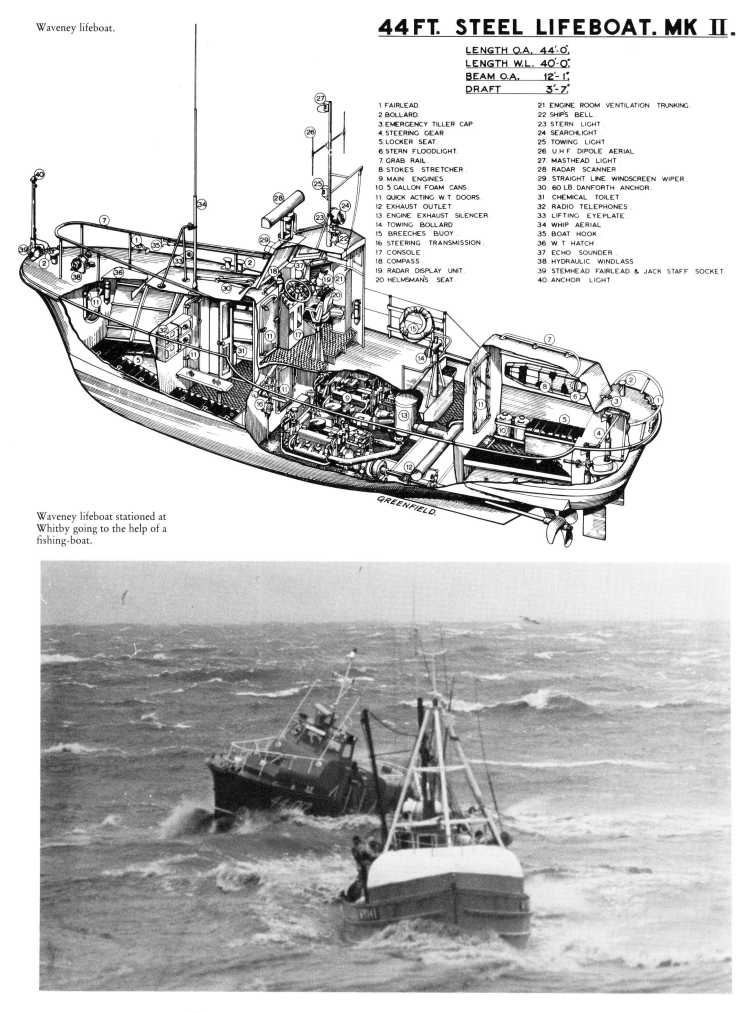

Waveney lifeboat stationed at Whitby going to the help of a fishing-boat.

was concerned this was only a fairly limited disadvantage: arguably with the advent of faster lifeboats more effective coverage could be given from the stations where the boats lay afloat and the need for some of the smaller and slower boats would be eliminated. The next two types of lifeboat to be designed for the RNLI were both boats which had to be kept permanently afloat.

One of these was the 50-foot Thames class lifeboat, similar in many respects to the Waveney. The other was named the Arun, the prototype being built at the yard of William Osborne at the mouth of the River Arun at Littlehampton. For the initial hull design of the Arun the RNLI turned once again to the Glasgow firm of G. L. Watson,

who assigned the task to Allen McLachlan, a former member of the RNLI's staff, who had already designed a small fast rescue boat.

An Arun boat was the first lifeboat to be specially designed for the RNLI with a glass-reinforced plastic (GRP) hull. The speed of 18 knots which was demanded of the designer was achieved. All controls and the electronic and navigational equipment were fitted in the superstructure. As a result, all crew members could visit any compartment they needed, without having to go out on deck. For rescue work close inshore a small inflatable boat was carried. The Arun was of course a self-righter.

Like other boats in the past, for example those designed by Beeching, by Watson or

One of the 460-horsepower Caterpillar diesel engines in the Arun lifeboat stationed at Torbay.

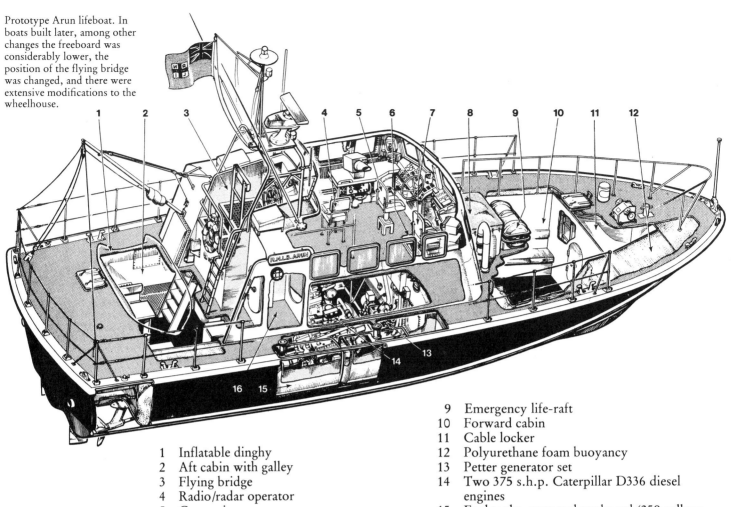

Prototype Arun lifeboat. In boats built later, among other changes the freeboard was considerably lower, the position of the flying bridge was changed, and there were extensive modifications to the wheelhouse.

1 Inflatable dinghy
2 Aft cabin with galley
3 Flying bridge
4 Radio/radar operator
5 Coxswain
6 Watertight hatch to forward cabin
7 Navigator
8 Rope stowage
9 Emergency life-raft
10 Forward cabin
11 Cable locker
12 Polyurethane foam buoyancy
13 Petter generator set
14 Two 375 s.h.p. Caterpillar D336 diesel engines
15 Fuel tanks, port and starboard (259 gallons each)
16 'Coffer dam' entrance to wheelhouse to prevent flooding if boat capsizes

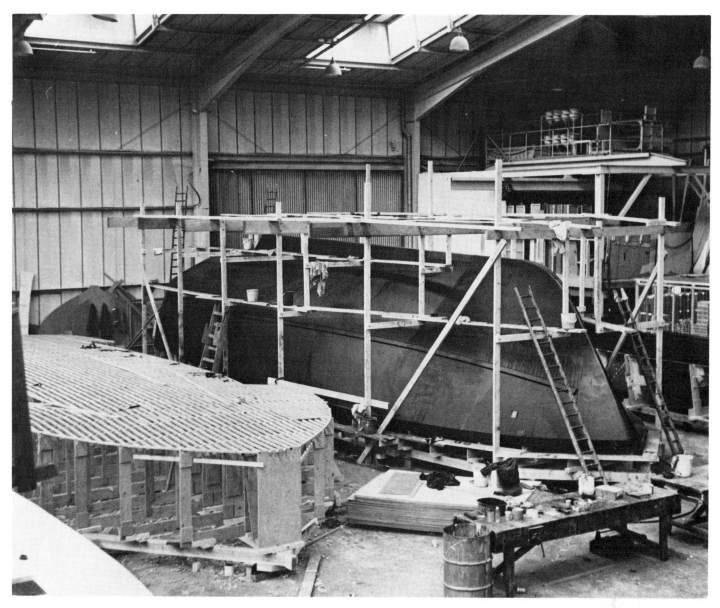

by Oakley, the Arun lifeboat may be thought to approach as near to perfection as the skills of her time permit. The greatly increased power and other qualities have enabled expert seamanship to succeed where it might otherwise have failed. The risk of capsize and the likelihood of the loss of a whole crew have been reduced. The Arun lifeboat was also greatly admired overseas after being shown at an international lifeboat conference which was held in Helsinki in 1975. But neither the hazards nor the discomforts of lifeboat service have been eliminated. The truth of all this became apparent in the winter of 1978–79 to a young coxswain named Brian Bevan.

In 1975 at the age of twenty-eight Bevan was appointed to an unusual post, that of coxswain superintendent of the Humber lifeboat station. This is the only RNLI station with a full-time crew living ashore. It is situated at Spurn Point, an inhospitable stretch of sand which offers virtually no

other form of employment. Four years later Bevan achieved a unique distinction. Medals awarded for gallantry during the preceding year are presented on the day of the RNLI's annual general meeting in London. In 1979 Bevan became the only man ever to have received the gold, the silver and the bronze medal at the same meeting. All three medals were for services carried out in an Arun lifeboat.

The bronze medal was awarded for a service to a Romanian cargo ship in a blizzard. The silver medal was for a rescue from a Dutch coaster. The coaster and the lifeboat crashed against each other three times before those on board the coaster, who included a twelve-year-old girl, could be taken off. The rescue for which the gold medal was awarded was from the motor vessel *Revi*, registered in Panama.

This was carried out on a February night in a force ten gale, extreme cold and intermittent snow showers. As the lifeboat made

opposite bottom and above
The prototype Arun lifeboats were built of wood, with the intention of passing on to GRP (glass-reinforced plastic) construction once the necessary lessons from the first prototype had been learnt. For the first of the GRP boats a wooden plug was prepared for the making of the mould. This is seen in the Halmatic factory in Havant, Hampshire.

for the casualty she crested a very large sea and crashed down some fifteen to twenty feet so hard that some of her electrical gear was seriously damaged. Her speed was reduced to a relatively modest 14 knots.

Brian Bevan had to bring the lifeboat a dozen times alongside the casualty. Everyone except the master had been taken off when the final run-in was made. As the lifeboat approached, the motor vessel's stem

rose twenty feet in the air and began to crash down on the lifeboat's foredeck, where the crew were lashed to the rails, with little, perhaps no chance of escape. Brian Bevan rammed the throttle full astern, and, in the words of the official report, 'the Arun's impressive power pulled her clear by only a matter of inches'.

The master of the *Revi* was taken off a few minutes before his vessel sank.

89

Saved by the St Ives lifeboat; a yacht in trouble in 1973.

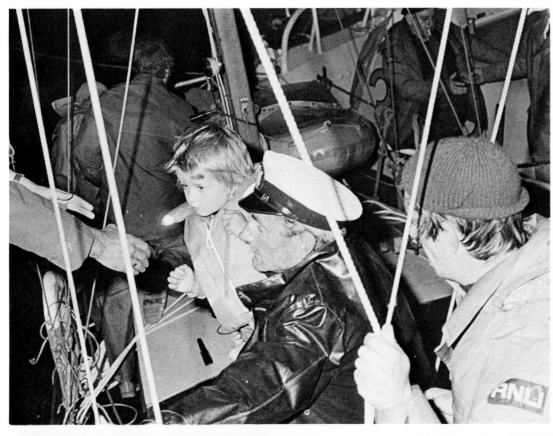

From horses to radar

For many years horses played an important part in the lifeboat service. At a number of stations the lifeboat cannot be kept afloat, either because there is no harbour or because the harbour dries out at certain states of the tide. In some places the lifeboat can be launched down a slipway, but this requires the presence of a pier on a rocky coast. At many stations therefore lifeboats had in the past to be propelled into the water by manpower, womanpower or horsepower.

On sloping shingle beaches it was possible to lay wooden skids over which the lifeboat could be eased, with large numbers of men and women pulling on ropes. At Dungeness in Kent, where the sea is steadily receding

and former lifeboat houses are to be found some distance inland, women helpers continued to operate the traditional launching methods well into the second half of the twentieth century.

On flat sandy beaches the lifeboat had, and still has, to be hauled into the water on a carriage, and for about a hundred years after the foundation of the RNLI horses were used for this purpose. Sometimes the haul was a long one. At Hoylake in Cheshire, for instance, the distance between high water and low water is approximately two miles.

The lifeboat horses, like the lifeboat men, had other forms of regular employment. Most of them were owned by local farmers

below
The crew at Porthoustock, Cornwall, about to launch on exercise in 1886.

opposite top
A launch by horses at Brooke, Isle of Wight.

opposite centre
Launch of the Whitby pulling lifeboat.

opposite bottom
Launching a tubular lifeboat for trials at Lowestoft in 1892.

Cresswell, Northumberland, where at one time women regularly helped to launch the lifeboat. In January 1876 a Swedish ship went aground near Newbiggin. Margaret Armstrong was one of a number of women who formed a human chain to try to bring survivors off the wreck. This failed, the lifeboat could do nothing because of the state of the tide, and a message had to be got to Newbiggin to ask the Coastguard to send the shore rescue apparatus. Margaret Armstrong and two other women set off through the gale and snow, but she alone had the strength to reach the Coastguard station, where she arrived with bleeding feet and almost speechless with exhaustion. Horses dragged the life-saving equipment to Cresswell, but by the time it arrived the lifeboat had successfully completed the rescue.

Women launching the lifeboat at Dungeness in the 1950s. At one time nearly all the launchers and nearly all the lifeboat crew at Dungeness belonged to two families, the Tarts and the Oillers, both of whom were believed to be of Huguenot descent and both of whom had depended for generations on fishing for their livelihood.

opposite
Hauling the Port Isaac lifeboat through the streets in 1927. The station was closed six years later but re-opened as an inshore lifeboat station with a small inflatable in 1968.

or railway companies, and some had to travel appreciable distances to the lifeboat station. At Hoylake one horse, on hearing the familiar sound of the maroons which called out the lifeboat, was reported to have become so excited that he had a heart attack and died.

There were other dangers too. In March

above
An early launching tractor
undergoing trials at
Hunstanton, Norfolk, in 1920.

right
Llandudno lifeboat being
hauled through the streets for
launching.

opposite
A rescue during the tragic
1979 Fastnet Race. This picture
shows the Courtmacsherry,
Co. Cork, lifeboat, which was
out for over 21 hours, with a
yacht in tow.

following pages
The Margate Rother class
lifeboat returns to her station.

1915, when the Bridlington lifeboat was being launched to go to the help of a mine-sweeper, a man named Robert Carr, who was riding one of the launching horses, was swept out to sea and drowned. Two of the horses were also drowned, and another rider escaped by being hauled into the lifeboat as she was carried past him.

It was largely through experience gained in the use of tanks in World War I that horses became redundant in the lifeboat service. The caterpillar tractor provided an obvious substitute, and the first trials with a tractor which could haul a lifeboat into the sea were conducted by the RNLI in 1920. Horses were used to launch a lifeboat for the last time at Wells in Norfolk in 1934.

Even with the use of a tractor, launching a lifeboat off a carriage into the sea continued to be a slow and painstaking procedure. At Llandudno in North Wales the lifeboat house is situated in the town some distance

from the launching point, and the sight of a tractor trundling through the streets with a lifeboat on a carriage in tow has understandably puzzled summer visitors. At St Ives in Cornwall local inhabitants have regularly complained that holiday-makers and their parked cars have impeded the passage of the lifeboat and carriage and so put lives at risk. Yet, laborious though the procedure is, so long as lifeboats are needed at places where they have to be hauled into the sea, and unless and until some better method is devised, launching by carriage and tractor must continue.

Like the caterpillar tractor radio-telephony was brought into service by the RNLI during the period between the two world wars. So long as communication was limited to flashing morse letters, semaphore, or amplified shouting it had to be accepted that while out on service a lifeboat, lying low in the water and often invisible in high seas, could be virtually out of contact with the shore, apart, that is, from the limited amount of information that could be con-

veyed by flares and rockets. This sometimes had tragic consequences.

In November 1928 the pulling lifeboat at Rye Harbour in Sussex was launched with a crew of seventeen when a message was received that a Latvian vessel was in distress. Soon after the launch it was learnt that the lifeboat was not needed, and recall signals were fired. These were not heard, and the lifeboat continued to search. Seas built up, and eventually the lifeboat returned. As she neared the harbour mouth she capsized in a following sea, and every member of the crew was lost. It was the greatest loss of life from any one lifeboat in the history of the RNLI, and it is probable that it would have been prevented if the recall signals had been received. The year before the disaster happened radio communication between lifeboat and shore was brought into operation for the first time.

The first form of radio communication was wireless telegraphy, a receiver and transmitter being fitted into the lifeboat at Rosslare Harbour in County Wexford in

opposite
Combined operation in the Channel Islands. On 14th July 1975 the tanker *Point Law* went aground on the extreme south-west tip of Alderney. The St Peter Port lifeboat, the Alderney fire brigade, a cliff rescue team, a French tug and a French helicopter were all involved before rescue was effected.

above
Boathouse and slipway at Tenby, the longest slipway in the British Isles. In the mid-twentieth century the RNLI began to face huge additional costs for the renovation, or even reconstruction, of a number of its older slipways. At some places the destruction of the pier meant that a new method of launching had to be adopted.

Launch by slipway at
Peterhead in a very rough
North Sea. Looking after the
fishing fleet is this station's
major job.

above
Lifeboat on slipway at Spurn
Point before the modern Arun
lifeboat, which lies afloat, was
placed on station.

opposite top
Centralized controls in a
Waveney lifeboat.

opposite bottom
The wheelhouse of an Arun
lifeboat.

1927. Telegraphy was soon superseded by radio-telephony, which had the obvious advantage of ease of operation and speed of communication. The first R/T sets were installed in 1929.

Radio equipment in lifeboats became more sophisticated in accordance with developments in the outside world. Medium frequency radios were supplemented by very high frequency and, for a time and for the specific purpose of communicating directly with helicopters, ultra high frequency sets. Advantage too was taken of new navigational aids.

The adoption of radar was delayed for some years because no radar equipment had been manufactured which could be of much practical use in a boat lying as low in the water as a lifeboat does. It was not until 1963 that the RNLI's first radar set was installed in the lifeboat at Yarmouth in the Isle of Wight. It was provided as a memorial to Joseph Conrad following an appeal launched by, among others, John Masefield, then Poet Laureate.

Echo sounders, radio direction-finding equipment and Decca navigators were also introduced in the years after World War II. For all these devices a place had to be found in existing lifeboats, and it was one of the evident merits of the US Coast Guard 44-foot boat, from which the Waveney developed, that in her the controls of engines and electronic aids were centralized. This led directly to the institution within the RNLI of the new post of coxswain-mechanic.

When motor lifeboats first came into service it was accepted that the coxswain, in command of the boat, should remain at the wheel and that another member of the crew, who came to be known as the mechanic, should operate the engines, taking his orders from the coxswain. As the maintenance of the engines was the most important task to be performed when the lifeboat was not out on service, it was the mechanic who normally became the one full-time member of the crew.

With the centralization of controls the

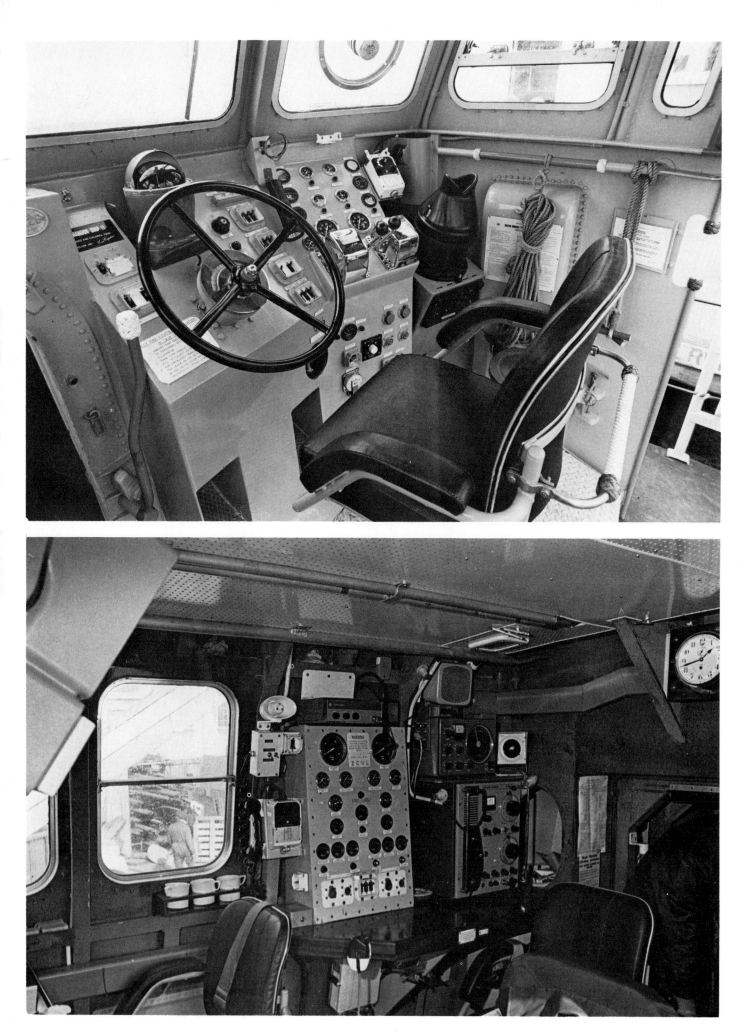

Curiosity.

Anxiety.

need for a separate crew member working the engines was obviated, and it was now the man in command, the coxswain-mechanic, who normally became the full-time crew member. This same system of centralized controls with a coxswain-mechanic in command was adopted in the Thames and Arun lifeboats.

Derek Scott, coxswain of the Mumbles

lifeboat in South Wales, a man of evident personal distinction, who has thought deeply about lifeboat problems and expressed himself with clarity, gave one of the most vivid descriptions in modern times of working conditions aboard a lifeboat in gales and heavy seas. He did this in a television interview in which he recalled how in November 1963 the Mumbles lifeboat

Consultation.

Decision.

Homecoming.

107

rescued the crew of ten from the Dutch motor vessel *Kilo*. The *Kilo* had a cargo of sodium drums, which caught fire in a force ten gale.

The distress call came about three o'clock in the morning, and to reach the lifeboat it was, in Derek Scott's words, 'a question of going along the pier on more or less your hands and knees at times to try to keep your footing'. He remembered the spray obscuring the lights of the lighthouse, which rose 180 feet above sea level, and encountering 'a wall of water which was about twenty feet thick'. The 45-gallon sodium drums were 'shooting up in the sky rather like Roman candles and then flopping in the water', and the sodium, as it came over the side of the ship, 'looked like boiling hot porridge'.

The Mumbles lifeboat was a Watson class boat built in 1947. In answer to the television interviewer, the playwright Colin Morris, Derek Scott said: 'Sophisticated navigation in an open boat when you are soaking wet is just not on. So you must remember the points on the way, taking bearings if you can see them.'

One of the principal merits of the Arun lifeboat is that a statement such as this, all too accurate though it was of the boat in which the rescue from the *Kilo* was carried out, would no longer be applicable. With the relatively spacious covered wheelhouse, skilfully placed controls and wheelhouse seats, to which all five members of the crew can strap themselves, sophisticated navigation in extreme conditions has been transformed from the virtually impossible to the merely difficult.

When Charles Fish spent the night standing by the *Indian Chief* in the open Ramsgate lifeboat in 1881 he fortified himself from time to time with a bite from a bar of chocolate. With the advent of electric kettles and self-heating tins, tea and soup became the most generally welcome forms of nourishment. Rum, which was replaced in the 1970s by brandy as a standard lifeboat supply, was accepted as being intended primarily for survivors and was seldom taken for other purposes. This may have been due to an instinctive understanding, which later studies of hypothermia confirmed, of the potential dangers of alcohol in extreme conditions of cold.

Rough weather launching of the Walmer lifeboat.

First aid treatment aboard Gorleston Atlantic class lifeboat by a female crew member. A small number of women serve as members of inflatable lifeboat crews, none as yet in the larger, conventional boats.

Dr Margaret Shimmin, honorary medical adviser of the Aith lifeboat station, with crew members. Aith, in Shetland, is the most northerly of all the RNLI's stations.

In putting forward his plans for a voluntary lifeboat service Sir William Hillary had suggested that the help of local doctors should be enlisted at the outset. In practice the RNLI was surprisingly slow to put this recommendation into effect. Lifeboat crews did take doctors out to ships if it was thought that their services might be needed. In World War II one doctor became almost an established member of the Walmer crew. This was James Hall, a courageous and ebul-

lient figure, whose published reminiscences, which eventually appeared in paperback form, called widespread attention to the services which doctors could perform when transported by lifeboat. Yet it was not until after World War II that the RNLI systematically enlisted medical help at all its lifeboat stations.

Much of what was then done was due to the quiet advocacy of Dr Geoffrey Hale, a member of the RNLI's Committee of

Protective clothing introduced in 1960, shown aboard Galway Bay lifeboat. This kind of clothing was before long superseded.

Admiral John Ross Ward, lifeboat inspector and inventor of a new type of lifejacket.

Management, who devoted nearly all the time he could spare from a general practice in the City of Westminster to the lifeboat cause.

Honorary medical advisers were appointed to lifeboat stations from among local doctors who were willing to put out in lifeboats when required. Instruction in first aid was given to volunteer crew members and certificates of proficiency issued. A new list of medical stores to be carried in lifeboats was drawn up, which eventually included morphine. Experiments were carried out with stretchers, survival bags, protective clothing and lifejackets.

In the provision of protective clothing the RNLI has tended to follow where others led. For decades lifeboat crews wore yellow oilskins which were colourful in appearance and which might be deemed to have romantic associations, but whose efficacy was limited. Derek Scott described accurately what happened to those who wore them. 'We were standing absolutely soaking wet from the water rushing through the neck of our oilskins, because we were dressed like the guy on a tin of sardines, and the boots used to fill up from the inside, so it was freezing cold.' It was not until some two decades after the end of World War II that the RNLI, as conservative in this respect as the fishing industry, introduced standard protective clothing which effectively kept the body dry.

In the design of lifejackets by contrast the RNLI did valuable pioneering work. In 1854 Captain (later Admiral) John Ross Ward, who held the post of inspector of lifeboats for thirty years, invented a new kind of cork lifejacket. The value of this became apparent when a lifeboat stationed at Whitby, which was locally administered and was not under the RNLI's control, capsized in 1861. The sole survivor, Henry Freeman, was the only man wearing the new kind of lifejacket which Ward had designed.

Kapok lifejackets were adopted in 1904.

Henry Freeman, the sole
survivor from the Whitby
lifeboat disaster of 1861.

Their efficacy was proved repeatedly, but because they were cumbersome to wear and impeded movement there was a dangerous tendency for crews not to wear them. In 1970 therefore the RNLI introduced its own new kind of lifejacket. This was in effect a self-righter, for it automatically brought a man face upright in the water no matter how he fell in. It was of a size and shape less liable to impair movement. Its inbuilt buoyancy could be increased by inflation by the mouth. Its fittings included a light, a whistle, a life-line, with which men could attach themselves to each other in the water while awaiting rescue, and a lifting becket.

Of the various devices which can be fired from a lifeboat the longest-serving is the line-throwing gun, which can project a line 150 yards to a casualty. One of the more colourful recent additions is the parachute

111

right
A cork lifejacket worn by David Hibbs, bowman of the Swanage lifeboat, around the turn of the century.

far right
Kapok lifejacket and medals worn by Captain William Watts-Williams, coxswain of the St David's, Dyfed, lifeboat. On 27th November 1954 the 20,000-ton Liberian tanker *World Concord* broke in two in a severe gale. One part drifted towards the Irish coast, the Rosslare Harbour lifeboat rescuing those aboard. Thirty-four men were aboard the other part, and to take them all off, the St David's lifeboat had to come alongside thirty-five times.

Lifeboat Inspector Dag Pike demonstrates a new type of lifejacket in 1967.

flare, which can dramatically, though briefly, illuminate a casualty and the surrounding water or rocks.

The Emperor Napoleon I wrote that in war moral considerations accounted for three-quarters, the other quarter being in effect the material. In the lifeboat service the ratio of importance between moral and material may be considered similar.

Those who over the years have provided the material for RNLI lifeboats, the inventors and designers, the craftsmen and manufacturers, the scientists and administrators, have laboured persistently, at times perhaps conservatively, but nearly always according to one recognized standard. This was to produce, not the most cost-effective, but the best. There has been a traditional belief within the RNLI, repeatedly enunciated, that those who are responsible for the material quarter must provide those who give the moral three-quarters with nothing but the best. It is an estimable ideal. It is also a policy which has been criticized by financiers in the past and, if maintained, can be expected to be criticized by financiers in the future.

An early method of throwing a line to a ship in distress, using a mortar. This system could only be used from shore.

Line-throwing gun demonstrated to Members of Parliament in 1924, during celebrations of the RNLI's centenary in London.

above
Firing practice with a
line-throwing gun at Cromer.

A selection of equipment carried in the modern
lifeboat

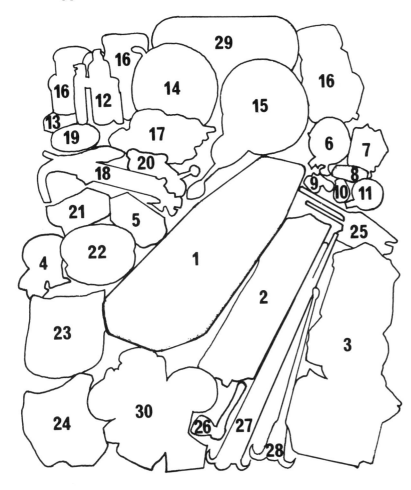

1 Stretcher – Stokes Litter type
2 Stretcher – Neil Robertson type
3 Lifeboatman's protective clothing
   (lifejacket, bump cap, jersey)
4 Lifelines
5 First-aid box
6 Searchlight
7 Line-firing apparatus
8 Flares
9 Binoculars
10 Torch
11 Loud-hailer
12 Fire extinguishers
13 Fire hose
14 Breeches buoy
15 Drogue
16 Ropes
17 Fenders
18 Anchor
19 Anchor float line
20 Heaving lines
21 Canvas carrying-sheet
22 Fresh-air breathing apparatus
23 Swimmer's lifejacket
24 RNLI ensign
25 Signalling flags
26 Axe
27 Boat hooks
28 Rope-cutting tool
29 Life-raft
30 Emergency provisions (including sweets,
   soup, brandy, cigarettes)

Coastguards and helicopters

In the mid-twentieth century a new type of rescue craft came into service whose usefulness for saving life at sea was comparable with that of the lifeboat. This was the helicopter.

The first successful use of a helicopter in helping to save life off the coast of Britain occurred in 1947. Three young miners had drifted out in a rowing boat off Prestwick. They were spotted from a helicopter which

The Dover lifeboat in a joint exercise with the rescue helicopter which was at one time operated by HM Coastguard at Manston.

opposite top
The German lifeboat *Hermann Ritter*. The larger German lifeboats are equipped with 'daughter' boats which are launched from the stern for carrying out rescues in shallow water.

opposite bottom
The Polish lifeboat *Monsun*. Poland is an active member of the international lifeboat organization and is regularly represented at conferences.

following pages
Sea King helicopter and Waveney class lifeboat stationed at Gorleston, cooperating in helping a survivor.

happened to be airborne. The position of the rowing boat was given to a trawler, which was able to rescue the miners. Ten years later the value of helicopters had been so clearly proved that the Royal Air Force decided to abandon its establishment of high-speed rescue launches, leaving only a few for such duties as target-towing.

By then the RNLI had set up its own sub-committee to investigate the use of helicopters. One of the early conclusions the committee reached was that the RNLI should not try to duplicate the efforts of the Royal Navy and the RAF by instituting a helicopter fleet of its own and that instead there should be close cooperation between service helicopters and lifeboats. This was in accordance with traditional RNLI practice.

From its earliest days the RNLI actively promoted the saving of life by vessels other than lifeboats. Small monetary payments, comparable with those given to members of lifeboat crews, were regularly made to people who put out from the shore in their own boats to rescue others, and claims for expenditure on fuel and other stores were met. In 1962, in an attempt to reduce the number of fatalities among those who put to sea in pleasure-craft, the RNLI and the Coastguard jointly drew up lists of boat-owners who might be called upon to try to

save life. Responsibility for operating this scheme and making payments to the boat-owners was soon afterwards accepted by the Coastguard. The RNLI's own direct answer to the problems posed by pleasure-boats was the inshore lifeboat.

Of the many people in Britain who have put out from the shore of their own accord in small boats to try to rescue others the most famous was certainly the daughter of the keeper of the Longstone lighthouse, Grace Darling. The story has been repeatedly told of the rescue from the steamer *Forfarshire* in September 1838, when Grace Darling, then aged twenty-two, and her father William rowed a coble to the scene of the wreck and saved the lives of nine people. It was never told more succinctly than by William Darling in the journal which he kept meticulously. In this he wrote much of the wreck, but of the part which he and his daughter played he confined himself to the statement: 'Nine others held on by the wreck and were rescued by the Darlings.'

The Darlings' coble was not of course a lifeboat or in any respect under the control of the RNLI. But it was fully in keeping with established policy that the RNLI – or the Shipwreck Institution, as it was then still called – should award its silver medal to both William and Grace Darling. To mark the

opposite
Oil rig *Orion* which went aground in Guernsey in February 1978 while in tow. The St Peter Port lifeboat and Royal Navy helicopters had earlier combined to rescue members of her crew in gale conditions at night.

Painting by James Carmichael of the famous rescue by Grace and William Darling in 1838.

The Coastguard station at Lowestoft. HM Coastguard is the co-ordinating body in the work of search and rescue at sea. On learning that a vessel is in distress, the coastguard immediately informs the honorary secretary of a lifeboat station, who decides whether the lifeboat should be launched. At sea the lifeboat maintains radio communication with the Coastguard station.

hundredth anniversary of the rescue the RNLI established a Grace Darling museum at Bamburgh under its own control. This housed the coble in which the rescue from the *Forfarshire* was carried out.

The governmental organization with which the RNLI has always been most closely linked is HM Coastguard. Members of the Coastguard service carried out a high proportion of the rescues effected round the coasts of Britain during the first twenty or thirty years of the RNLI's existence. They won one-third of the total number of awards for gallantry made by the RNLI between 1824 and 1852. Many of these were for services in lifeboats, and the number of such awards began to drop only when an instruction was issued to lifeboat stations that those who served in the Coastguard should no longer be enrolled as primary members of lifeboat crews but only as auxiliary members. The duties of the Coastguard ashore were judged to be too important to be neglected while a lifeboat was out on service.

Most of these Coastguard duties which were in danger of being neglected were concerned with the protection of the revenue. Although today it serves exclusively to promote safety and rescue at sea, the Coastguard grew out of the old Coast Blockade, which was formed in 1817 largely to combat smuggling.

As a preventive force it was one of the more widely disliked public bodies. Nor was it particularly effective, for smuggling in Britain in the nineteenth century was virtu-ally eliminated not by preventive measures, but through the introduction of free trade. It was therefore understandable that a number of those engaged in the preventive service should also undertake more gratifying tasks. During a four-year period of duty in Fifeshire a Coastguard officer named Lieutenant Randall rescued no fewer than thirty people from the sea.

Control of the Coastguard alternated between the Board of Trade and the Admiralty, for there were some who believed the Coastguard's main value might be to provide a reserve of manpower for the Royal Navy in the event of war. Indeed it was not until 1925 that the Coastguard was divested of a variety of subsidiary duties and left with two clearly defined functions. One was to provide an adequate coast-watching service. The other was rescue from the shore by life-saving apparatus.

The use of shore-based rescue apparatus developed from two inventions which occurred almost simultaneously early in the nineteenth century. One was the discovery by an imaginative naval officer, Captain George Manby, that with the use of a mortar he could fire a line over Downham church in Norfolk. The other was a means of propelling a line by rocket or cylinder and was the invention of Henry Trengrouse of Helston in Cornwall. Once a method of firing a line with reasonable accuracy to a vessel on the rocks had been discovered the use of such rescue devices as the breeches buoy followed.

Volunteer shore-rescue teams have regularly cooperated closely with lifeboat crews. Some of the teams were for a time under the RNLI's control, one at Aberdeen remaining so until it was transferred to the Coastguard in 1965. Their tasks and the conditions in which they have to operate may be no less onerous than those of lifeboatmen.

The visual watch kept by the Coastguard was supplemented in time by radio, and it is from a combination of the two that a lifeboat station receives the great bulk of the information on which it is required to act. The Coastguard has a duty to inform a lifeboat station that the services of the lifeboat may be needed and can request a launch. The decision to launch or not rests with the honorary secretary of the station or, in his absence, his appointed deputy. The Coastguard has similar links with the Royal Navy and the RAF and while a rescue service is being carried out acts as the coordinating body. On the receipt and passage of accurate

Rescue by Blyth volunteer shore rescue team of HM Coastguard by breeches buoy from SS *Holderness*.

information by the Coastguard much of the success of modern air-sea rescue inevitably depends.

The Coastguard and the armed forces are not the only governmental or other public bodies with which the RNLI has to work closely in the interests of safety and rescue at sea. In 1897 wireless signals were first successfully transmitted from shore to a ship eighteen miles away under the direction of Guglielmo Marconi. Two years later the first distress call ever to be transmitted at sea

Interior of HM Coastguard station at Wells, Norfolk.

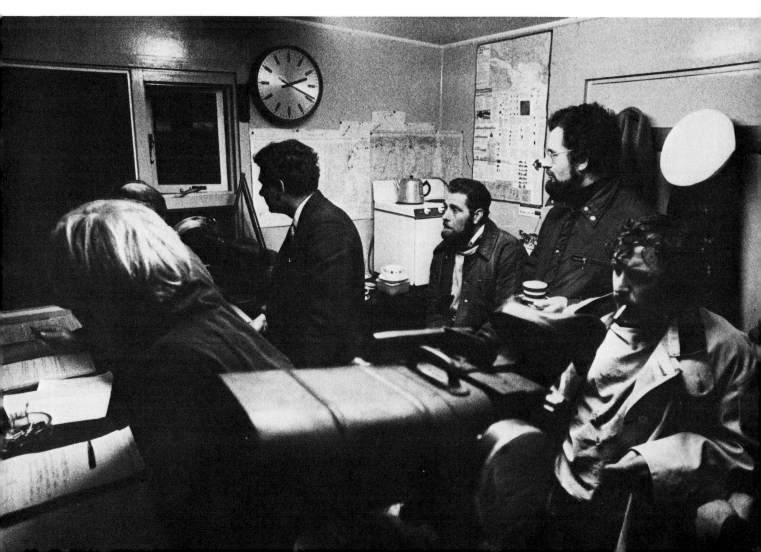

Yarmouth, Isle of Wight, lifeboat delivers Christmas fare to Needles lighthouse.

was sent out from the East Goodwin light-vessel, which had been rammed by a steamer.

To prevent uncontrolled morse signals being transmitted on a variety of wavelengths an Act of Parliament was passed in 1904 which brought radio-telegraphy in the United Kingdom under the control of the Postmaster-General. In time the Post Office established a chain of radio stations for handling traffic with ships in all parts of the world.

Lighthouses and lightvessels round the coasts of England and Wales are controlled by the Corporation of Trinity House, a body which grew out of a guild of mariners which was established at Deptford in Kent and to which Henry VIII granted a charter in 1514. Lighthouses and lightvessels in Scotland and the Isle of Man are controlled

by the Commissioners for Northern Light-houses; those in the Irish Republic and Northern Ireland by the Commissioners of Irish Lights. Local authorities have respon-sibilities for beach safety measures, and when an examination of beach safety was conducted in the 1970s the sponsoring government department was the Home Office.

With such a multiplicity of bodies con-cerned with safety and rescue in coastal waters the question may reasonably be asked whether efficiency might not be im-proved if one organization were given responsibility for all aspects. To this ques-tion more than one answer can be given.

In the hypothetical case of a country with no organization for rescue at sea, an evident need to establish one and ample financial resources, the best model to emulate might

Brought ashore by Coastguard at Fraserburgh.

well be the US Coast Guard, which, in addition to other duties, provides a comprehensive air-sea rescue service.

In Britain different bodies have grown up concerned with different aspects of safety and rescue, each with its own operational expertise, traditions and management skills. To replace them all by one single body would be wasteful and destructive. To bring them under centralized control would probably result in little more than the creation of a new and fairly thick upper layer of bureaucracy.

In the 1960s a need to integrate policies more closely was, it is true, increasingly felt, largely because of the growing complexity of the rescue services. To meet this a Search and Rescue Committee, on which the different organizations concerned were represented, was set up in 1971 under the aegis of the Department of Trade and Industry. This pragmatic solution of a limited problem was probably as satisfactory as any likely to be devised.

The Royal Air Force began building boats for the specific purpose of rescuing airmen who came down in the sea in 1935. The number of RAF high-speed launches in commission during the Battle of Britain in 1940 was still pitifully small. Wartime advances served to increase greatly the knowledge of survival techniques. Experiments were made with new devices, such as an airborne lifeboat invented by a well-known yacht designer, Uffa Fox, who had served his apprenticeship in a drawing office alongside Richard Oakley. But it was with the post-war development of the helicopter, largely through the skills of a US citizen of Russian origin, Igor Sikorsky, that the RAF began to play a major role in rescuing civilians as well as servicemen from the sea. Concurrently with the RAF the Royal Navy developed its own helicopter fleet.

The early helicopters in service in Britain could not operate more than about sixty miles from their base. Their carrying capacity was limited to six or seven, and they had several operational limitations at night, in fog and in exceptionally severe winds. To compensate for these they had considerable advantages over the lifeboat in speed and

Medallists at RNLI annual general meeting in 1955: on the right US helicopter pilot Captain Curtis E. Parkins and his crew.

ability to search an area. They could also at times effect rescues from vessels which lifeboats could not reach.

This was vividly brought to public attention during a prolonged period of severe gales in November 1954, when the South Goodwin lightvessel broke from her moorings, began to drift and was found lying on her beam ends on the sands. There was one survivor aboard, a twenty-two-year-old bird-watcher in the service of the Ministry of Agriculture and Fisheries. No lifeboat could come within 150 yards of the lightvessel, and the bird-watcher was rescued by a helicopter piloted by Captain Curtis E. Parkins of the US Air Sea Rescue Squadron stationed at Manston in Kent. Captain Parkins was the only pilot of an aircraft ever to receive a medal for gallantry from the RNLI.

With the advent in Britain, albeit in small numbers, of Sea King helicopters many of the earlier shortcomings were eliminated. Nevertheless lifeboats and helicopters remained, and seem likely to remain in future, complementary rescue craft.

opposite
Rescue of two fishermen by an RAF helicopter off Wells, Norfolk, in 1977.

In August 1979 two deepening depressions sweeping in from the Atlantic brought severe gales rising at times to storm force and hurricane. During this period the Fastnet Race, a yacht race from Plymouth, around the Fastnet Rock off the south coast of Ireland and back again, took place. A massive combined search and rescue operation had to be mounted. It was coordinated by the Marine Rescue Coordination Centre at Shannon in the Irish Republic and HM Coastguard at Land's End.

Helicopters of the Royal Navy, the Royal Air Force and the Irish Air Corps, RAF Nimrod aircraft, naval vessels, merchant ships, fishing vessels and yachts all took part. A Netherlands warship acted as guardship for the racing fleet.

Thirteen RNLI lifeboats put to sea and saved the lives of 60 people; 74 were rescued by helicopter. The whole operation showed how, for all the complexity of the organization involved, coordination of action can be achieved. It also showed lifeboats and helicopters fulfilling, as they should, their complementary roles.

Lifeboats
of other nations

In the pamphlet which he published in 1823 Sir William Hillary stated emphatically that lifeboats should go to the help of the people and vessels of all nations 'as well in war as in peace'. Other lifeboat organizations adopted the same code, and the principle is now agreed that in saving life at sea no distinctions are made on grounds of nationality or race, creed or colour.

This international obligation, accepted on behalf of crews, has been accompanied by a free exchange of information between the lifeboat organizations of different countries. There has also been a general readiness to provide guidance and expertise wherever they have been needed.

The two Dutch lifeboat societies, whose separation from each other has a purely geographical basis, have always had a particularly close affinity with the RNLI. They too are financed solely by voluntary contributions. Whereas the main strength of the RNLI has been derived from a multiplicity of local branches, the strength of the Dutch societies has traditionally come from individual members. A membership scheme comparable with that of the Dutch was adopted by the RNLI only in the second half of the twentieth century.

In a number of other European countries the RNLI has had an important influence, both by example and direct assistance, in the

Wartime damage. The lifeboat house and lifeboat at Tynemouth were destroyed by a direct hit by a German bomb on 9th April 1941. Although RNLI lifeboats put out on service 3760 times during World War II, only three lifeboatmen were killed by direct enemy action.

128

creation of lifeboat services. In France the establishment of the body which came to be known as the *Société Centrale de Sauvetage des Naufragés* was ordered by the Emperor Napoleon III in 1865 to coordinate the work of the existing local lifeboat stations. It was accepted that the RNLI should serve as a model.

In Germany, following the loss of the whole crew of a ship off Borkum in 1860, two Germans living near Bremen, a lawyer and an instructor of navigation, made a public appeal for the creation of a national organization similar to the RNLI.

The lifeboat organization of imperial Russia sought the advice of John Ross Ward, the lifeboat inspector and inventor of the RNLI lifejacket, and in recognition of his service its Patroness, the Grand Duchess Cesarevna, presented him with a silver and crystal model of a droshky. He was also given, at the end of his visit to Russia, a certificate which stated in English: 'Your name will ever be intimately associated with the humane work to which you have devoted so many years of your life.'

After World War I another RNLI inspector spent some time in Romania as the guest of the lifeboat society there. In Spain it was decided in 1971 to reorganize the lifeboat service under a new name, *Cruz Roja del Mar*. Two new RNLI lifeboats visited Spain at the request of the new society and completed their evaluation trials there. One of them effected a successful rescue from a

Spanish trawler aground in fog. When it was agreed, also after World War II, to create a rescue organization in Switzerland, with more than seventy boats operating on the lakes, it was to the RNLI that the organizers came for their principal guidance.

The influence of the RNLI has also been apparent in the widespread tendency among European nations to establish and maintain their lifeboat organizations as voluntarily financed bodies. In some European countries, Belgium and Denmark among them, the lifeboat services are wholly controlled by the State. Elsewhere, as in Norway, money accepted from the Government, at first for restricted purposes, has led to steady official encroachment. But in several countries the preference for the voluntary system has been as explicitly stated as it has been in Britain.

After World War II the lifeboat service in Western Germany was re-established with Government assistance, but in 1957 the *Deutsche Gesellschaft zur Rettung Schiffbrüchiger* informed the Government of the German Federal Republic that it no longer needed help from the State and wished to revert to the voluntary system. This was in effect a repetition of the decision made by the RNLI in 1869.

Fifteen years after the German reversion to a voluntary lifeboat service the *Svenska Sällskapet för Räddning af Skeppsbrutne*, the lifeboat society of Sweden, acted as host at a conference of voluntary lifeboat

20-knot inflatable lifeboats of the Spanish *Cruz Roja del Mar*.

organizations which met at Malmö. The delegates unanimously expressed their belief in 'the overwhelming advantages of the voluntary system for the provision of an efficient and economical service'.

Outside Europe the most influential body engaged in saving life at sea is, and has long been, the US Coast Guard. The first organization in the United States for rescuing life in coastal waters of which any records are known to exist was the voluntary Humane Society of Massachusetts. It began to provide shelters on the coast for shipwrecked mariners in 1789 and established a lifeboat station at Cohasset in 1807.

The Humane Society's sphere of operations was limited. The long and sparsely inhabited coastline of the United States lacked the numerous small towns and villages from which in Europe voluntary lifeboat services have grown. It was therefore logical that a duty to save life at sea should be entrusted to official bodies, the Revenue Marine and later the US Life Saving Service.

Although the US Coast Guard is of greater antiquity than the US Navy, the modern form of the Coast Guard may be said to date from 1915, when the Revenue Cutter Service and the Life Saving Service were amalgamated. The new body became in time responsible for lighthouses and lightvessels, buoys and beacons, weather ships and ice-breakers, patrol boats and amphibious helicopters and a highly sophisticated world-wide reporting system, whereby the position of any vessel of any nationality included in the system can be plotted at any time in any part of the world. The lifeboat fleet manned by full-time, uniformed servicemen is one unit in a very much larger complex.

No other country has an organization concerned with life-saving which is comparable in size and variety of responsibility with the US Coast Guard. But in the Western Hemisphere it has been natural, when plans have been formulated for establishing some kind of service for rescue at sea, for the planners to turn to the US Coast Guard for guidance and example. This has happened for instance in Canada.

The US Coast Guard includes a voluntary element known as the Coast Guard Auxiliary, which provides education, guidance and examination for boat-owners as well as a pool of volunteer rescuers and patrollers. When the establishment of some similar body was envisaged in Australia in the 1970s it was to the US Coast Guard Auxiliary, and not to the RNLI, that the organizers turned in search of a suitable model.

The first formal international lifeboat conference took place in 1924. It was held in London as part of the celebration of the hundredth anniversary of the RNLI's foundation. The major public attraction was described by the RNLI as something 'never

International service. This photograph of the Margate lifeboat was taken by a cadet serving on board the German training ship *Pamir*.

held before – an international pageant of lifeboats'. Included in the procession on the Thames were a steam lifeboat and a twin-screw lifeboat from the Netherlands, a sailing lifeboat from Norway, a Swedish 'full sail and motor' lifeboat and motor lifeboats representing Denmark, France and the RNLI.

During the conference Count Yoshii, President of the Imperial Japanese Lifeboat Society, moved a resolution, which was carried unanimously, calling for the formation of 'an international lifeboat organization on the lines of the Red Cross Society'. It was agreed that copies of this resolution should be sent to all maritime countries and to the League of Nations.

George Shee, the Secretary of the RNLI, did have discussions at the headquarters of the League of Nations in which he represented the eight countries whose delegates had attended the London conference. Nothing of consequence seems to have emerged, and the lifeboat organizations of the world, fortunately perhaps, were left to conduct their own affairs without interference.

The second international conference of

US Coast Guard cutter on patrol in ice-infested waters.

131

lifeboat services was held in Paris in 1928, when 17 nations were represented. From then onwards, apart from a gap caused by World War II, conferences have been held at four-yearly intervals. It also became accepted practice that discussions at international lifeboat conferences should be conducted in the English language.

The setting of the conference held in 1951 was Brussels, and it was there that the RNLI was formally requested to undertake the task of distributing information to all countries with lifeboat organizations and therefore, in effect, to provide the central lifeboat secretariat. In recognition of this distinction the RNLI placed on the outside

132

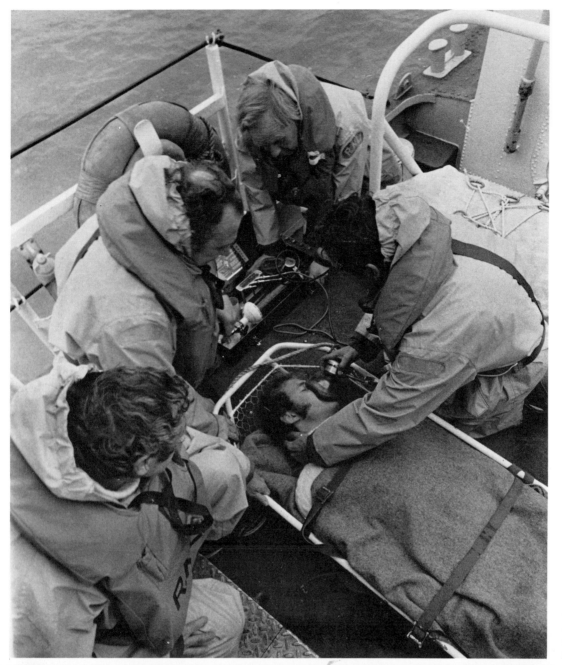

A stretcher case handled aboard the Harwich, Essex, lifeboat.

Lifeboats of several nations visited Plymouth in 1974 to mark the 150th anniversary of the RNLI's foundation.

133

of its head office building in Grosvenor Gardens in London a plaque bearing the words 'Permanent Headquarters, International Lifeboat Conference'. This was later transferred to a new RNLI head office building at Poole in Dorset.

The annals of the lifeboat organizations of the world are replete with records of rescues and attempted rescues from vessels of other nations. Not infrequently men have lost their lives on such missions. When the Southport and St Anne's lifeboats capsized in 1886 they were going to the help of a German vessel. When the whole of the crew of the Rye Harbour lifeboat were lost in 1928 the ship in distress was Latvian. Brian

The wreck of the *Hindlea*. For the rescue of the crew of the 500-ton coaster in October 1959 Richard Evans received his first gold medal for gallantry. He rated the rescue a more exacting one even than the later rescue from the *Nafsiporos*. It was carried out in a lifeboat of the reserve fleet, with a crew of five instead of the normal seven. One of the five, Hugh Jones, had never been out on operational service before. Gusts of over 100 mph were recorded, and the lifeboat had to make ten separate runs-in before the coaster's crew of five could be taken off.

Bevan won his three medals in rapid succession in the winter of 1978–79 for services to a Dutch, a Panamanian and a Romanian vessel.

In December 1966 a service was carried out off the north-west coast of Wales which led to the award of two gold medals for gallantry. The vessel in distress was Greek, namely the 1287-ton steamer *Nafsiporos*.

In a full north-westerly gale the Holyhead lifeboat put out under the command of her coxswain, Thomas Alcock. On board was the inspector of lifeboats for the area, Harold Harvey, who happened to be attending a meeting near Holyhead when the distress call was received.

In the course of the rescue Coxswain Alcock made a decision which required some moral courage. He asked Harold Harvey to take the wheel and, therefore, command of the boat and himself took charge of the rescue party on deck. A second lifeboat, which also put out to help, was under the command of Coxswain Richard Evans, who already held the gold medal for gallantry.

The two lifeboats found the *Nafsiporos* rolling to an angle of 35 degrees among waves which were sometimes 35 feet from trough to crest. Wind speeds were recorded of 100 miles an hour. Aboard the *Nafsiporos* a ship's boat was hanging loose from a davit, and with no common language the lifeboatmen could not explain to the crew of the Greek steamer that the boat must be cut away from the falls.

As the Holyhead lifeboat came alongside the crew's fears were confirmed. The loose boat continued to sway, broke loose and finally crashed on to the deck of the lifeboat. By extraordinary chance nobody was hurt, and in combination and, as the two men in command, Harold Harvey and Richard Evans, later indicated, a certain rivalry the Holyhead boat and the Moelfre boat successfully completed their missions.

Richard Evans was brought up in the Welsh-speaking village of Moelfre, where his grandfather was coxswain of the lifeboat. He himself went to sea in coasters, and on his first voyages he was reluctant to go ashore because of his limited knowledge of English. Yet in spite of this apparent handicap he was to reveal, when speaking the English language, gifts as an orator comparable with his gifts as a seaman.

For a long time Richard Evans was the only man alive to have won the RNLI's gold medal for gallantry twice. After he retired from lifeboat service he was retained by the RNLI as a lecturer, holding audiences in many parts of Britain and Ireland riveted as he described the conditions of service in a lifeboat.

His greatest triumph as a speaker came in 1974, when the Corporation of the City of London gave a dinner in the Guildhall to mark the 150th anniversary of the RNLI's foundation. Richard Evans was asked to reply to the toast of the RNLI. As soon as he had finished Sir Alec Rose, the round-the-world yachtsman and a dedicated voluntary worker for the RNLI, stood up to applaud. Others followed, and a standing ovation was given of a kind seldom before experienced in the Guildhall.

Richard Evans made numerous appearances on television. When he became the subject of the programme *This is Your Life* the Greek captain of the *Nafsiporos*, among others, had an opportunity of expressing his gratitude. He was also the subject of a successful biography. This was appropriately entitled *Lifeboat V.C.*

Another man whose fame in an earlier age was comparable with that later acquired by Richard Evans also achieved much of his

Canadian rescue hovercraft, believed to be the first vessel of its kind employed primarily on rescue duties.

The three principal figures involved in the medal service in 1966: Coxswain Richard Evans of Moelfre (gold medal), Lifeboat Inspector Harold Harvey (gold), Coxswain Thomas Alcock of Holyhead (silver).

distinction by rescuing seamen of other nations. This was Henry Blogg of Cromer, who was awarded more medals for gallantry than any other man in the history of the RNLI. A number of his greatest exploits took place in time of war.

On the morning of 9th January 1917 the small Greek steamer *Pyrin* hoisted a distress signal, and the Cromer lifeboat crew assembled. Henry Blogg, who was the coxswain, was in his thirties, but because of the demands of war most of his crew were older men. Their lifeboat was a pulling and sailing boat, which was launched off the beach.

The launch was a difficult one, and the help was needed of a number of soldiers who were stationed in Cromer. For a long time the lifeboat could make little headway, but eventually she reached the Greek vessel and took off her crew of sixteen.

As the lifeboat reached the shore a tremendous explosion occurred aboard a Swedish ship, the SS *Fernebo*. One of her boilers burst, and the force of the explosion broke the ship in two. She was loaded with timber, and this had the strange effect of allowing the two parts of the ship to drift away from each other, with neither of them listing or even settling in the water.

Although her crew were exhausted by the long struggle to reach the *Pyrin* the Cromer lifeboat put out again. For half an hour the crew struggled to bring the lifeboat beyond the breakers, but they failed repeatedly and were driven back on to the shore.

The two parts of the *Fernebo* ran aground, and it seemed likely that rescue could now be effected by rocket apparatus from the shore. All attempts failed, and Henry Blogg decided that the lifeboat must put out again.

There was another long struggle through the breakers. Five oars were broken, three more were washed ashore, and the lifeboat, after running dangerously near the shore, was again driven back.

Spare oars were now produced, and the lifeboat crew decided they must make another attempt. This time they succeeded, and all eleven men known to be still on board the *Fernebo* were rescued.

Nearly twenty-four years later, in another world war, the Cromer lifeboat, still under the command of Henry Blogg but now a motor lifeboat, rescued eighty-eight men from a convoy of six ships which had gone aground on the Happisburgh Sands.

In two world wars crews of the RNLI repeatedly fulfilled the obligation accepted by Sir William Hillary of going to the help of peoples of all nations 'as well in war as in peace'. There was also one major operation in which lifeboats took part which was arguably outside the scope of their humanitarian task. This was the evacuation from Dunkirk

above
Lifeboat gold medallists in 1924. Left to right: John Swan of Lowestoft, Henry Blogg of Cromer, William Fleming of Gorleston, Robert Smith of Tynemouth, John Howells of Fishguard, Major H. E. Burton of Tynemouth.

opposite
Henry Blogg of Cromer, the winner of more medals for gallantry than any other man in the service of the RNLI.

in the summer of 1940. Two of the lifeboats, those from Margate and Ramsgate, were manned by their normal crews. The others were commandeered by the Royal Navy.

With so much at stake and the survival of Britain as a free nation in grave doubt the niceties of whether lifeboats should or should not take part in what was clearly a military operation were understandably given little attention. Nor has the question ever been debated at international lifeboat conferences.

The question of the status of lifeboats in any war of the future has however been considered more than once. One proposal put forward has been that lifeboats should be given official recognition under the Geneva Convention comparable with that of units of the Red Cross. A prime advocate of this has been the chief administrator and, later, chairman of the Swedish Lifeboat Society, Hans Hansson, a former Lord Mayor of Gothenburg, a dominant figure at international lifeboat conferences and the man who convened the conference of voluntary lifeboat societies which was held in Malmö in 1972.

Hansson's advocacy of a special status for lifeboats under the Geneva Convention has tended to be listened to with polite but limited interest. Yet he may well prove to be a pioneer of a policy which will one day gain general acceptance. It would certainly be consistent with the resolution passed at the thirteenth international lifeboat conference held at The Hague in 1979, when it was agreed that support should be given to an application for the award of the Nobel Prize for Peace to the International Lifeboat Conference.

Indeed it may not be too fanciful to envisage the ultimate task of lifeboats in the event of a nuclear war. It could conceivably be that of ferrying a few survivors to remote islands or other places believed to be still uncontaminated. Such a task, gruesome though it would be, would conform with all the best traditions of the Royal National Lifeboat Institution and those of the other lifeboat services of the world.

The RNLI~ facts and figures

Modern lifeboat profiles

44' WAVENEY
(steel with aluminium superstructure)
Introduced 1967
Length overall 44' 10½"
Beam 12' 8"
Draft 3' 11"
Displacement 18 tons
Maximum speed over 15 knots
Range at full speed 167 nautical miles
Crew 5

54' ARUN
(wood or GRP)
Introduced 1971
Length overall 52' and 54'
Beam 17'
Draft 5'
Displacement 28.30 tons
Range at full speed 220 nautical miles
Crew 5

50' THAMES
(steel with aluminium alloy superstructure)
Introduced 1973
Length overall 50'
Beam 14' 6"
Draft 4' 8"
Displacement 23.5 tons
Maximum speed 17 knots
Range at full speed about 200 nautical miles
Crew 5

48' 6" SOLENT
(steel)
Introduced 1969
Length overall 48' 6"
Beam 14'
Draft 4' 7"
Displacement 27 tons
Maximum speed over 9 knots
Range at full speed 240 nautical miles
Crew 7

37' 6" ROTHER
(wood)
Introduced 1973
Length overall 37' 6"
Beam 11' 6"
Draft 3' 1"
Displacement 13 tons
Maximum speed over 8 knots
Range at full speed 150 nautical miles
Crew 7

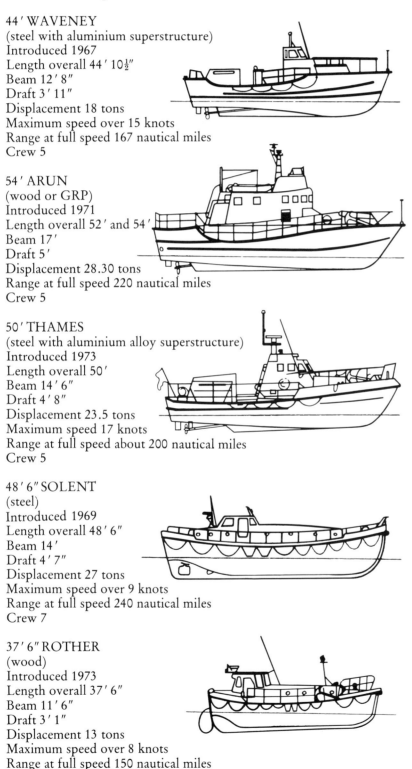

The Royal National Lifeboat Institution was founded in 1824 with the purpose of saving life at sea. It is a registered charity, and is entirely funded by voluntary contributions. Its function is to provide, on call, the 24-hour lifeboat service necessary to cover search and rescue requirements to 30 miles out from the coasts of the United Kingdom and the Republic of Ireland.

The fleet
The RNLI has an active fleet of about 260 lifeboats. Of these about 120 are high-speed inflatable boats. There is also a relief fleet of some 60 lifeboats. There are 200 lifeboat stations in the UK and Eire.

Lives saved
In 1979, there were 2569 lifeboat launches (an average of seven a day). There were 1008 lives saved. Since the foundation of the RNLI, its lifeboats have saved over 105,000 lives.

Organization
The RNLI's headquarters is at Poole, Dorset, where the administrative, operational and fund-raising staff are located, and rescue and station personnel records are kept. Technical staff deal with the design and construction of new lifeboats and modification of existing ones. A design studio and flag-day and souvenir store handle display and fund-raising requirements. There is also a depot with a store of spare parts, and a machine shop manufacturing special items for lifeboat maintenance. Lifeboats are sent to commercial boatyards for regular overhauls to keep them in top condition.

The RNLI has eight operational divisions, but the day-to-day running of each station is left to the local voluntary committee, run by an honorary secretary whose duties include the authorization of each lifeboat launch. Usually the only fulltime employee of the station is the mechanic, who deals with day-to-day maintenance of the boat.

Each station also has an honorary medical adviser who may go on the lifeboat if a doctor is required by a vessel. The RNLI awards medals in bronze, silver and gold for outstanding gallantry.

Lifeboat stations in 1980

DEREK SCOTT (Mumbles)
'On a bad night with the slates coming off the roofs, the telephone wires down and a big sea running, I know how the crew feel. I've felt it myself. But bad weather is what we're prepared and trained for.'

KEITH BOWER (Torbay)
'It was probably more difficult for my wife than for me. I had a job to do all the time, whereas she could only contemplate the hazards we were facing.'

MATTHEW LETHBRIDGE (St Mary's)
'Grandfather . . . he was coxswain before Dad; and my Uncle Jim and Dad were both in the lifeboat with him. At one time, Dad was coxswain, my uncle was second coxswain, I was the bowman and my two brothers, Harry and Richard, and my cousin, James, were in her as well.'

STEPHEN WITTLE (Dunmore East)
'You always think that you're going to master the sea, but no, you must always respect the sea. It's always the mighty one, it'll win in the end, no matter how you try.'

CHARLES BOWRY (Sheerness)
'I look for people who fit in. I don't always go for the big hefty blokes. Sometimes a weedy little guy who looks as if he wouldn't say boo to a goose can go out and battle a storm with the best of them.'

JOE MARTIN (Hastings)
'One day you'll be battling with fog for 22 hours, looking for survivors and just as you're frozen stiff and giving up hope you spot them. Just the look on their faces when they realize they're not going to die. That's enough.'

Index

The author and publishers would like to thank the photographers, newspapers and agencies, many of whom, in addition to
giving their time to take the photographs, have waived their normal fees for this book; Symington Macdonald and Alan Neal
for reading the text and making a number of helpful suggestions; Rosalind Smalley and Marjorie Gifford for typing; Richard
Wilson, Tony Argent and Ray Tredwen of Kodak Ltd. whose sponsorship of the photographic exhibition 'In Danger's
Hour' inspired this book; Heather Deane, who first suggested the book; Ray Kipling for help with picture research; and the
RNLI, its lifeboat crews and station officials for their patient co-operation.